First Gear

MYTH-BUSTING MOTORING MILESTONES
First Gear

KEITH RAY

The

First published 2019

The History Press
97 St George's Place, Cheltenham,
Gloucestershire, GL50 3QB
www.thehistorypress.co.uk

British Library Cataloguing in Publication Data.
A catalogue record for this book is available from the British Library.

ISBN 978 0 7509 8816 2

Typesetting and origination by The History Press
Printed in Europe

Contents

Introduction

My objective in writing this book was to establish a timeline of global 'firsts' in the history of automobiles and motoring in general. However, identifying 'firsts' is always fraught with problems. The main problem is deciding what we actually mean by a 'first'. Do we mean:

- When the idea was first mooted?
- When a patent was first applied for?
- When the first patent was awarded?
- When the first working prototype was made?
- When an innovation first found its way into production?
- When the innovation first appeared in mass production?

The answer is rarely clear cut. Take, for example, disc brakes. The first disc brakes on a production car appeared as early as 1902 on Lanchester cars. However, they were not very successful as they were made of soft metal and were quickly worn away by the dust and grit thrown up from the poorly made early roads. Disc brakes were later developed for use on aircraft, where they became very successful. Such brakes would not appear again on a car until after the Second World War when the weird and wonderful Crossley Hot Shot was launched with disc brakes on the front wheels. The first car with discs all round was the 1953 Austin-Healey 100S, but that was a limited-production high-performance model: only fifty were made. The first mass-production car fitted with discs was the Citroën DS which, from 1955 until the model ceased production twenty years later, had inboard discs at the front which remained unchanged throughout its 1.5 million production run.

The other problem with identifying proper 'firsts' is what we might call the 'persistent myth', where a mistaken attribution becomes so much part of popular culture that correcting the mistake may become completely impossible. Perhaps the worst case of a persistent myth concerns the diesel engine. The simple truth is that it was not invented by Rudolph Diesel! The myth is so persistent that his name has been linked to the design for over 120 years. This type of engine was actually invented by an Englishman, Herbert Akroyd Stuart (1864–1927), who first patented the 'diesel' engine in 1886, and by 1890 Richard Hornsby & Sons of Grantham, Lincolnshire was mass-producing Akroyd Stuart's compression-ignition oil engines. This was a full three years before Rudolph Diesel had filed a single patent. By 1892 Akroyd Stuart had developed a high-compression version with the fuel injected directly into the cylinders, just as in modern 'diesel' engines. By contrast, Diesel's first engine in 1897 blew a mixture of fuel and air into the cylinder and did not have direct injection. In any case, Diesel's fuel initially was not oil but rather finely powdered coal. One of these early coal-dust engines exploded and Diesel was almost killed. There were lengthy legal actions by Akroyd Stuart and Hornsby-Akroyd against Rudolph Diesel, which lasted right up until Diesel's apparent suicide in 1913.

So in compiling my timeline of 'firsts' I have tried to take a balanced view, mentioning where appropriate conflicting claims of origin. Of course, no timeline of this sort will ever be perfect and free from flaws, and some of the attributions and dates may be disputed by some. Along the way I have highlighted where significant myths have clouded the history of automobiles and motoring, and attempted as far as is possible to correct these. In some instances, it has been appropriate to 'carry forward' inventions and highlight some of the later, most significant, applications.

It seemed very appropriate to make 'the first car' the opening section of the book. Indeed the issue of 'what was the first car' is itself the first 'myth buster'!

Nineteenth-Century Firsts

1803: THE FIRST AUTOMOBILE

The generally accepted wisdom is that the first automobile was the one built by Karl Benz in 1885. But is that correct? To a large extent it depends upon what is meant by the word 'automobile'. The word derives from the Greek 'auto' meaning 'self', and the French 'mobile' which simply means 'moveable'. So presumably an automobile is just something that can move itself... which is not particularly helpful! However, there were several self-propelled vehicles before 1885 which could claim to be the first automobile. For example, in 1769 Nicolas-Joseph Cugnot built a self-propelled steam-powered vehicle which could carry people and things. However, with a vast boiler slung out front, it was completely unstable, and the boiler and furnace needed to be cleaned out and re-fired every fifteen minutes. On its first journey it careered out of control and demolished a wall. So I don't think that counts! Then in 1801, Cornishman Richard Trevithick built a successful steam-powered motor

1803 Richard Trevithick's second steam carriage (Courtesy of Barry Herbert)

vehicle which could carry eight people and attain 8.4mph. He demonstrated it on the streets of his native Camborne. Buoyed by his success, Trevithick built a second carriage in 1803 which he drove all the way to London. That was definitely an automobile!

I accept none of these in any way resembles what we understand today as an automobile, but neither did Benz's three-wheeled carriage. There have been plenty of successful steam-powered cars over the years, such as Stanleys and Whites, so an internal-combustion engine is not a critical part of the definition of a car. Given that fact, Richard Trevithick certainly has a very valid claim to have built the first automobile. So the automobile age started in 1803!

And what about petrol-engined cars? As we shall see later, Benz was also beaten to this by both fellow German Siegfried Marcus in 1870 and by Frenchman Édouard Delamare-Deboutteville in 1883.

1813: THE FIRST BY-PASS

Archway Road in North London is arguably the world's first by-pass. Built in 1813, it was constructed to avoid the congestion in the village of Highgate and make the climb up Highgate Hill easier for horses. The road had been planned as a tunnel, but it collapsed during construction and so was opened up as a cutting with Nash's celebrated archway carrying the Hornsey Road overhead. In the early days, of course, it was home to just horse-drawn and steam-powered vehicles, but it was subsequently used by cars with internal-combustion engines as part of the Great North Road. It is still in use today, and can fairly claim to be a 'first'.

1886 Benz (Chris 73 CC SA 3.0 via Wikimedia Commons)

Reigate tunnel built 1823 (Ian Capper CC 2.0 via Wikimedia Commons)

1823: **THE FIRST ROAD TUNNEL**

The world's first road tunnel also predates the modern automobile but was used by cars right up until the 1970s as part of the A217 road. It was built in 1823 by Earl Sommers who owned a house on top of the hill in Reigate and wanted to stop traffic passing through his estate.

1845: **THE FIRST PNEUMATIC TYRES**

Everyone knows that the pneumatic tyre was invented in 1888 by John Dunlop. The only problem is that Dunlop did not invent the pneumatic tyre! It is more accurate to say he reinvented it forty-three years after it was actually invented by another Scotsman, Robert William Thomson, who filed his patent on 10 December 1845. However, Thomson's tyres never made it into production, although he successfully demonstrated their advantages of greater comfort and reduced noise. In order to promote his invention, Thomson arranged a public demonstration of his tyres in 1847

London's Regent's Park. Thomson didn't use the term 'tyre' for his invention, preferring the more fanciful 'aerial wheels'. It seems pneumatic tyres must have had a special fascination for Scottish men in the nineteenth century because the first *practical* pneumatic tyre was made in 1888 by the Scottish-born John Dunlop, owner of a veterinary practice in Belfast. Dunlop had a very specific purpose in developing his tyre. His son used to ride his bicycle on the very rough roads of the day, and Dunlop believed the extra comfort afforded by the pneumatic tyre would prevent his son getting the headaches he used to suffer. Dunlop patented his tyre on 31 October 1888, but this patent referred only to bicycles and light vehicles. There were some legal problems because of Thomson's earlier work, which had been patented, but Dunlop managed to overcome these problems. Working with an inventor by the name of Charles Kingston Welch, he set up their Pneumatic Tyre Company, which would later become Dunlop Tyres.

1860: THE FIRST DUAL CARRIAGEWAY

The term 'dual carriageway' is generally accepted as meaning a road with the carriageways for traffic travelling in opposite directions separated by a central reservation. Typically, they have two lanes in each direction, roads with more lanes generally being classed as motorways or freeways. It is likely that dual carriageways are more ancient than most people realise. As with many things in life, the Romans may have got there first! The Via Portuensis, built in the first century AD and linking Rome to its sea port appears to have been a dual carriageway for some of its length, although it is not known why. In 1860, just prior to the ascendancy of motor cars, Savery Avenue in Carver, Massachusetts was constructed with a narrow strip of trees down the centre, although this was probably more to do with aesthetics rather than safety. A good candidate for the title of the first modern dual carriageway is the Long Island Motor Parkway, which was opened in 1907. This was in part a dual carriageway, with around one-fifth of its length having the traffic separated by a central island, again probably mainly for aesthetic reasons.

Surprisingly, once the motor car had become established in the 1910s and 1920s, dual carriageways remained rare. It was not until the 1930s that they became much more popular. The dual carriageway is popularly associated with the Art Deco period, and the development of suburbs in the 1930s.

1861: THE FIRST SPEED LIMITS

The world's first speed limits were introduced in 1861 in the United Kingdom. However, predating these limits was the United Kingdom Stage Carriage Act 1832, which first introduced the offence of endangering the safety of a passenger or person by 'furious driving'. However, no precise number was placed on the speed classified as 'furious'. The UK's Locomotive Acts of 1861, 1865 and 1878 are generally recognised as the first quantification of speed limits. The first of these Acts in 1861 imposed an overall limit of 10mph on the open road, and a reduced limit of 4mph in rural areas and just 2mph in towns. Today many motorists in Central London would be grateful to be able to drive as quickly as 2mph! In 1896 the Locomotives on Highways Act raised the speed limit to a breathtaking 14mph. Reflecting the original Stage Carriage Act of 1832, 14mph was assumed to be the speed of a horse being driven 'furiously'.

1868: THE FIRST PEDESTRIAN CROSSING

The world's first purpose-built pedestrian crossing was installed at the corner of Bridge Street and New Palace Yard off Parliament Square in London in December 1868. It was designed specifically to make it easier for members of parliament to cross the road to reach the Houses of Parliament, presumably so they didn't miss crucial votes having remained in the local hostelry for a little too long!

1868: THE FIRST TRAFFIC SIGNALS

The first pedestrian crossing also brought about the world's first traffic signals, installed in December 1868 just after the crossing had been installed. Mounted on a 22ft cast-iron pillar at the site of the pedestrian crossing, the signal was the invention of J.P. Knight, a railway signalling engineer, and it looked very much like a railway signal with a hand-turned revolving lantern, semaphore arms and gas-operated red/green lamps for use at night. The lights were manually operated, requiring a policeman to be on duty all the time. The first traffic lights were not popular with the general public, and were the subject of much derision. It must be remembered that in the 1860s traffic, even in big cities, didn't really conform to lanes, and so the signals probably increased confusion and congestion rather than reduced it. These lights remained the only traffic lights in the world until they were removed not long afterwards, having blown up and killed the policemen on signal duty. This discouraged any further development of traffic signals until the era of motor cars truly began, and indeed traffic lights were not reintroduced to London for another fifty years. Most motorists in London think there are far too many!

1869: THE FIRST FLYOVER

What is generally considered the first 'flyover' in the world was constructed in London. Between Newgate Street and Holborn there was a deep dip in the road, which was part of the Fleet Valley. The Fleet River itself had been enclosed underground as early as 1737, but the valley still remained and was a serious obstacle for horse-drawn traffic. Built between 1863 and 1869, the Holborn Viaduct enabled the traffic to avoid the need to descend and then ascend the steep valley sides. Queen Victoria opened it in 1869, and it is still in use today.

1869: THE FIRST CAR ACCIDENT

In 1869 an Irish scientist called Mary Ward was riding in a steam-powered automobile built by her cousins. As they rounded a bend too quickly, Ward was thrown from her seat and fell into the path of the vehicle. One of the rear wheels rolled over her and she was killed instantly. If we limit the definition to petrol-powered vehicles, then the first road accident was probably in the city of Ohio in the United States. In 1891 an engineer by the name of James Lambert was driving one of his home-made cars when it hit a tree root sticking out of the ground. Lambert lost control of the vehicle and it swerved and crashed into a post. Lambert and his passenger suffered only minor injuries.

Holborn Viaduct opened 1869 (Matt Brown CC 2.0 vvia WIkimedia Commons)

1870: THE FIRST PETROL-ENGINED CAR

Although Karl Benz is generally credited with constructing the first automobile, his 1886 creation wasn't only not the first automobile, it wasn't even the world's first petrol-engined vehicle. In 1870 a fellow German by the name of Siegfried Marcus installed a two-stroke petrol engine on a pushcart, and over the next few years built four progressively more sophisticated internal-combustion-engined cars including, in 1880, a vehicle with a four-stroke petrol engine. Then in 1883, Frenchman Édouard Delamare-Deboutteville built a vehicle powered by a petrol engine to replace the horse transport used at his father's cotton mill. Helped by his father's mechanic, he modified an 8hp stationary engine and mounted it on a four-wheeled hunting-brake. The vehicle no longer exists, but Édouard's design drawings for it do.

Whilst these vehicles were one-offs, they certainly merit being called 'cars'. However, in fairness to Karl Benz, he did begin what we would call the motor industry. His first vehicle was a three-wheeled two-seater with a 0.75hp single-cylinder four-stroke engine mounted horizontally at the rear. His 1886 patent for his 'vehicle powered by a gas engine' may be regarded as the birth certificate of the automobile industry ... but he wasn't the first with a car!

1879: THE FIRST STREET LIGHTING

Street lighting predates the modern motor age, of course. So we need to look at both the very first street lighting and also the first street lighting of the automobile era, which was around 1879. The world's very first street lighting appeared in 1807 as a demonstration of the concept in Pall Mall in London, installed by Frederick Albert Winsor. It was a success and led to the creation of the London & Westminster Gas Light & Coke Company under a Royal Charter issued in 1812. It is believed this was the world's first dedicated gas company. In 1814, street lighting was also installed on Westminster Bridge, and the lights we see today on the bridge recall the original design. Moving towards the motor-car age, arc lights enjoyed a brief popularity but were very high maintenance, produced a very glaring light and were very unpopular. It was the incandescent light bulb, invented independently and simultaneously by Joseph Swan and Thomas Edison, which came to illuminate the roads at night for the early motorists. The first street in the world to be lit by these bulbs was Mosley Street in Newcastle upon Tyne in 1879, making Newcastle the world's first city to be lit by modern street lighting. After 1879, street lighting quickly began to spread across the UK and the rest of the world.

1885: THE FIRST 4X4

Most people believe that 4x4s started with Land Rovers and Jeeps during the 1940s. In fact, four-wheel-drive vehicles have been around since the very dawn of road travel, and even pre-date the petrol engine. The very first four-wheel-drive vehicle of any sort is believed to be a traction engine built in 1885 by the English firm of Fowler & Co. In terms of automobiles, the first can be claimed by Ferdinand Porsche who, in 1899, designed a four-wheel-drive electric vehicle for Hofwagenfabrik Ludwig Lohner & Co. of Vienna.

This car was also one of the very earliest hybrids, driven by electric motors in all four wheels and powered by batteries, which were in turn, charged by a petrol generator.

1886: THE FIRST DASHBOARD

Today the word 'dashboard' means the place in the car where we find all the instruments, most of the controls as well as heating vents, glove boxes and 'entertainment modules'. But the origin of the 'dashboard' is very different from what we understand today. The original function of a 'dashboard' was to protect the drivers of horse-drawn vehicles, carriages and sleighs from mud, stones and debris being thrown up by their horses' hooves. These boards, which were designed to prevent the stones 'dashing' against the coachman, were usually made of wood and leather. The very first cars were three-wheelers, with a single wheel at the front. With this format it was difficult to include a dashboard, but when four-wheeled vehicles appeared the dashboard returned with its original function. The first car dashboard was on the 1886 Daimler shown in the photograph. The Oldsmobile Curved Dash, which

1889 Lohner Porsche four-wheel drive

1886 Daimler (Enslin CC SA 3.0 via Wikimedia Commons)

was the first mass-produced motor car, derived its name from the curved 'dashboard' similar to those found on horse-drawn sleighs.

1886: THE FIRST DIESEL ENGINE

As we saw in the introduction, Rudolph Diesel did not invent the engine which falsely carries his name. It was an Englishman, Herbert Akroyd Stuart (1864–1927), who first patented the 'diesel' engine in 1886, and by 1890 Richard Hornsby & Sons of Grantham, Lincolnshire was mass-producing Akroyd Stuart's compression-ignition oil engines a full three years before Rudolph Diesel had even filed a single patent. Akroyd Stuart's engines found their way into a variety of road vehicles, mostly tractors, but it would not be until the 1930s that 'diesel' engines small enough and light enough to be used in cars would appear.

1886: THE FIRST FOUR-WHEELED CAR

The very first cars had only three wheels, with a single steerable wheel at the front. The very first four-wheeled car appeared in 1886, the product of Gottlieb Daimler. Daimler knew a lot about internal-combustion engines but little about cars as such, having had thirteen years' experience of building engines at the Deutz engine works. Leaving Deutz in 1882, he set up in business with Wilhelm Maybach, who had been a colleague at Deutz. By 1883 Daimler and Maybach had built their own first engine, a high-speed petrol unit, and in 1885 they installed one firstly in a motorcycle and then later in a horse-drawn carriage. This engine was a single-cylinder unit which could run at 700rpm, seen as 'high speed' back in 1885. This is generally accepted as being the first four-wheeled car in the modern sense.

1888: THE FIRST PETROL (GAS) STATION

Petrol (gasoline) was first sold to the public at pharmacies or chemists shops. However, the petrol was just seen as a sideline to their core business. It is believed that the very first such 'filling station' was in Germany in the town of Wiesloch, where the city pharmacy began selling petrol in the late 1880s. When Bertha Benz took delivery of her first automobile in 1888 she stopped in Wiesloch on her way from Mannheim back home to Pforzheim to fill up. Since 2008 this event has been commemorated by the annual Bertha Benz Memorial Route event.

The world's first purpose-built 'gas station' opened in St Louis, Missouri in 1905. This was followed two years later by the second purpose-built facility in Seattle in Washington State. This was operated by Standard Oil of California, now part of Chevron. Once Henry Ford started mass-producing 'affordable' cars for the American middle class, the demand for filling stations mushroomed across the States.

1889 Daimler V-twin (Herranderssvensson CC SA 3.0 via Wikimedia Commons)

1889: THE FIRST 'V' ENGINE

The very first 'V' engine of any sort for a car was a two-cylinder V-twin built by Daimler in 1889 to a design by Wilhelm Maybach. This 'first' would eventually give rise to V4, V6, V8, V12 and even a few V16 automotive engines. Volkswagen even produced a V5 in 1997. The V format has the advantage of generally being more compact that the equivalent 'straight' engine, a benefit which increases the more cylinders there are. In a V-formation, the addition of two cylinders only adds one 'bore' to the engine's length, whereas in a straight format two 'bores' are added. The photograph shows one of the 1889 V-twin Daimler engines, which is on display at the Musée de l'Aventure Peugeot, Sochaux.

1890: THE FIRST CAR HEATERS

A Canadian, Thomas Ahearn, takes credit for the first electric car heater in 1890. His heater used a fan to exchange warm air between the engine compartment and the interior of the car. It was pretty basic, potentially dangerous should there be an exhaust leak and had just two settings: on and off. In the early 1900s there was an alternative to the electric heater in the form of a 'heater box'. These were simple, squat, fabric-covered metal boxes into which hot bricks could be inserted. The passengers could then warm up their feet and legs on them. Although crude they offered some protection from the freezing cold in early open cars. Later, engineers realised a lot of heat was going to waste from the engine, and initially manifolds around the exhaust pipes were used to funnel warm air into the car. By the 1920s, cars were being sold which used the circulating cooling water passing through a small radiator where a fan would project the heat into the car. This was the birth of the modern car heater, and the basic design has hardly changed.

1891: FIRST CAR IN SERIAL PRODUCTION

Although the Model T Ford may lay claim to being the first car made on an assembly line (which actually is not even true! See '1902'), several cars were in serial production much earlier. A lot

1891 Peugeot Type 3

depends upon what we understand by 'serial'. The Peugeot Type 3, launched in 1891, had a production run of sixty-four, which probably counts as 'serial'. A rival claim is the later 'curved dash' Olds launched in 1901, which claimed to be the first car to exceed an output of ten per week. In the first year 433 examples were made, and the total produced rose to 5,508 in the first three years. Its popularity was due to its being very much cheaper than its competitors.

1893: FIRST FOUR-WHEEL STEERING

In 1987 Honda made a big thing about the four-wheel steering on their Prelude model. Many manufacturers had been grappling with the concept for years before, but Honda came up with their simple levers-and-rods approach and claimed a 'first'. Now whilst the Prelude may have been the first petrol-engined car to sport four-wheel steering, it certainly was not the first road vehicle to have it. That crown goes a steam traction engine with four-wheel steering built in 1893 by English engineer Bramah Joseph Diplock. This Tasker engine was also one of the first vehicles ever to have four-wheel drive. The rather low-quality photograph is one of only two known to exist. As well as four-wheel drive and four-wheel steering, this amazing vehicle also had independent suspension on all four wheels.

1901 'curved dash' Olds (Alf van Beem CC 1.0 via Wikimedia Commons)

1893 Diplock Tasker traction engine with four-wheel steering

1893: FIRST VEHICLE REGISTRATION PLATE

The first registration plates appeared in France in 1893. The Paris Police Ordnance of 14 August 1893 stated that, 'Each motor vehicle shall bear on a metal plate and in legible writing the name and address of its owner, also the distinctive number used in the application for authorisation. This plate shall be placed at the left-hand side of the vehicle – it shall never be hidden'. Initially the Ordnance only applied to Paris, but in 1901 the rule was extended across the whole of France. The next country to introduce registration was Germany in 1896.

1894: THE FIRST AUTOMATIC TRANSMISSION

Everyone knows that automatic transmission was invented by General Motors and made its debut as Hydra-Matic as an option on 1940s Oldsmobiles. Except that, like so many things that 'everyone knows', this is not correct! The very first crude automatic transmission, based on centrifugal weights to change gear, was built in 1894 by Frenchmen René Panhard and Émile Levassor. However, the system was crude and unreliable, and progressed no further. The first successful automatic transmission was invented in 1921 by a Canadian steam engineer by the name of Alfred Horner Munro of Regina in Saskatchewan. He applied for and received a patent for a compressed air-based transmission in 1923, and whilst it was reliable it didn't find a commercial outlet. The real leap forward came in 1932 from Brazil when José Braz Araripe and Fernando Lehly Lemos developed an automatic transmission using high-pressure hydraulic fluid. They managed to interest General Motors in their idea, and they sold the prototype and the design to GM

1940 Oldsmobile (Sicnag CC 2.0 via Wikimedia Commons)

who introduced the technology in the 1940s Oldsmobile model as 'Hydro-Matic' transmission. However, there is still controversy. An article in the *Wall Street Journal* credits the German auto parts company ZF of Friedrichshafen with the invention shortly after the First World War.

1894: THE FIRST STEERING WHEEL

The first automobiles were steered using a tiller, but in 1894 Alfred Vacheron took part in the Paris–Rouen race in a Panhard 4hp model, which he had fitted with a steering wheel. It is believed this was the first application of a wheel to steer a car. However, this was a one-off experiment. Of course, wheels had been used for many years for large steam vehicles, such as traction engines and steam rollers, but for light cars a tiller was seen initially as more appropriate. Starting in 1898, all Panhard et Levassor cars were equipped as standard with steering wheels, making them the first production cars so equipped.

1894 Panhard et Levassor 4hp (Alf van Beem CC 1.0 via Wikimedia Commons)

1895: THE FIRST COIL SPRINGS

The very first car to feature coil springs was the 1895 Daimler, although it only had coils at the rear. The Daimler was the work of Wilhelm Maybach who worked for Gottlieb Daimler. The Riemenwagen, as the car was called, was a carriage-like automobile with a rear-mounted engine whose power was transmitted to the wheels

1910 Brush Runabout (Donated by Nordiska Museet)

1895 Daimler

by belts. The car was fitted with various versions of Maybach's 'Phoenix' twin-cylinder engine. Around 150 examples were made, and although the Riemenwagen never decidedly influenced the development of automotive engineering, it still has a firm place in history as it was used as the world's first petrol-engined taxi. The first car to make use of coil springs all round was the Brush Runabout, made from 1910 to 1913. The Runabout was a light car with a chassis of wooden rails and iron cross members, friction-drive transmission

and 'underslung' coil springs in tension instead of compression. Coil springs did have one drawback compared to leaf springs. Leaf springs are 'self damping' in that when the leaves rub together when flexed they induce a damping effect which coil springs lack.

1895: THE FIRST MOTORING ORGANISATION

It did not take long for early motorists to form clubs of like-minded people. The world's first motoring organisation was the Automobile Club de France, which was founded in 1895. Interestingly, early motoring in France had been popular with keen cyclists, and it was a group of former racing cyclists who formed the club. This was followed later in the same year by the American Motor League, whereas Britain's RAC was not formed until two years later in 1897.

1896: THE FIRST CAR MASCOT

The first ever car mascot is believed to be the St Christopher that Lord Montagu's father commissioned in 1896 for his new Daimler. Interestingly, the Rolls-Royce Spirit of Ecstasy, the most famous car mascot, is believed to have been modelled on Eleanor Thornton, who was secretary to Lord Montagu's father. The most highly coveted mascot is probably the rearing elephant found on the bonnet of the ill-fated Bugatti Royale, designed by sculptor Rembrandt Bugatti, brother of Ettore. Rembrandt finished the original bronze in 1903, but it was only after he committed suicide in 1916 that six were made in tribute, to decorate the endless bonnet of his brother Ettore's 'folie de grandeur'. The inspiration for mascots often came from nature, as with the leaping cat, designed for Jaguar by the doyen of motoring artists F. Gordon Crosby, and Alvis's crouching hare. Women in various states of undress were popular too!

1896: THE FIRST ELECTRIC STARTER

Prior to the invention of electric starters, car engines were started by a variety of methods. These included gunpowder cylinders, wind-up springs and, of course, the starting handle. Using a starting handle was difficult, inconvenient and potentially quite dangerous. If the engine 'kicked back' there was a serious danger of the motorist's hand being badly injured. Advice at the time, often ignored, was to place fingers and thumb below the handle. However, it was natural to grip the starting handle with the thumb above it, which – should the engine 'kick back' – lead to broken thumbs or worse. In addition, with increasingly larger engines with higher compression ratios, hand-cranking became much more difficult and dangerous. The very first electric starter was a retro-fit on an Arnold car, which was basically an adaptation of a Benz Velo. Mr H.J. Dowsing, an electrical engineer living in East Peckham in the UK, fitted the starter to his car in 1896. Seven years later, in 1903, Clyde J. Coleman filed a patent for the first electric starter in the US. The first serial production of cars with electric starters fitted as standard began in 1912 at both Lanchester in England and Cadillac in the US.

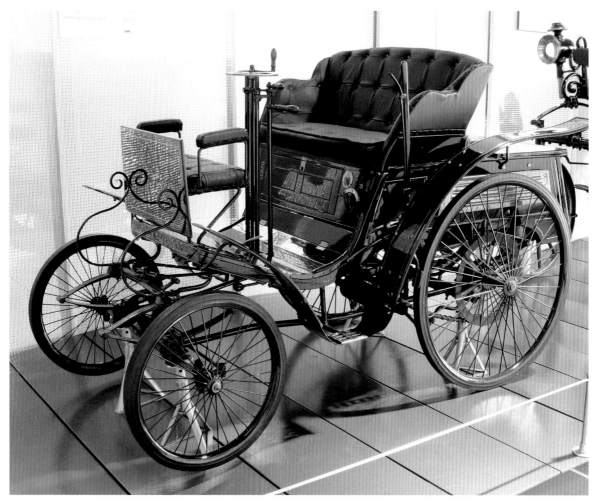

1896 Arnold (Softeis CC 3.0 via Wikimedia Commons)

1896: THE FIRST SPEEDING FINE

The first person in the world to be convicted of speeding was the very same man who installed the first electric starter. Yes, it was the same Walter Arnold of East Peckham! On 28 January 1896 he was charged with driving at 8mph, which was four times the urban speed limit of 2mph. He was fined just 1s. That is equivalent to just £4.63 today, so he got off rather lightly. Today he would have been more likely to have been prosecuted for driving too slowly, which can be an offence in its own right. However, today four-times the urban speed limit of 30mph would be 120mph, so I suspect today that offence might result in rather more than just a fine.

1896 Peugeot Type 5

1895: THE FIRST STOLEN CAR

The world's first ever reported theft of a car is believed to be that of the 1895 Type 5 Peugeot belonging to Baron de Zuylen. The dastardly deed took place in Paris in June 1896 when the Baron's car was back at the Peugeot Freres' factory for repair. The perpetrator broke into the factory and stole the vehicle, but fortunately for the Baron his car was recovered and the thief was caught. There is no record of the fate of the thief. The photograph is of a nicely restored Type 5 Peugeot in the Musée de l'Aventure Peugeot in Sochaux, France. This car was of the 'tête-à-tête' design where the driver and his passengers sat opposite each other, which didn't do a lot to help the driver's view of the road!

1897: THE FIRST DRUNK DRIVING CONVICTION

On 10 September 1897 a 25-year-old London taxi driver named George Smith became the first person ever arrested for drunk driving after slamming his cab into a building. Smith later pleaded guilty and was fined 25s, equivalent to a mere £116 today. Like Walter Arnold the year before, Smith also got off lightly without even a ban!

1897: THE FIRST TAXIS

The world's first motorised taxis were electric, powered by batteries rather than petrol engines. Electric taxis appeared in both London and New York in the same year: 1897. In London, Walter C. Bersey introduced a fleet which became nicknamed 'hummingbirds' on account of the sound they made. At around the same time in New York, the Samuel's Electric Carriage & Wagon Company began running a fleet of twelve electric hansom cabs, a fleet which grew to sixty-two by 1898. The world's first petrol-engined cab was built by Gottlieb Daimler in 1897 and began plying for business in Stuttgart the same year. Given

that Daimler would become Daimler-Benz, the nickname of lower-range Mercedes as 'Stuttgart Taxis' was as appropriate in 1897 as today! This taxi also incorporated the first 'taximeter', invented by Friedrich Wilhelm Gustav Bruhn, Friedrich Nedler and Ferdinand Dencker, which automatically calculated the fare. Petrol-engined cabs appeared in Paris in 1899, London in 1903 and New York in 1907.

The number of taxis increased very rapidly around the world in the early twentieth century. After the invention of the taximeter, the next big

First taximeter (Sargoth CC 1.0 via Wikimedia Commons)

innovation was the use of two-way radios, which appeared in taxis in the late 1940s. These enabled the taxi driver to communicate with his base without having to stop to use a public telephone, thereby serving his customers more efficiently.

1897: THE FIRST CAR INSURANCE POLICY

In the earliest days of motoring there were very few cars, and those that were on the road were slow. After the First World War the automobile started to become a common sight in many countries. By that time cars were much faster and, as a result, potentially much more dangerous, yet nowhere in the world was there any requirement for compulsory insurance. Some people took out voluntary insurance to cover themselves in the event of an accident. It is believed that the very first car insurance policy was taken out by a certain Gilbert L. Loomis, a resident of Ohio, in 1897 with the Travellers Insurance Company. Although strictly it was written as a 'horse & carriage' policy, it did cover Loomis in the event he hurt someone or damaged property whilst driving his car. But with no compulsory insurance, injured victims would seldom get any compensation after an accident and drivers often faced considerable bills for damage to their cars and property.

1898: THE FIRST DRIVING SCHOOL

It is commonly believed that driving schools and driving lessons began in the first decade of the twentieth century. In the UK, the first official driving lesson was given in 1910 near Peckham in south London by Stanley Roberts, a doctor's son. Realising driving would soon become big business, Roberts set up a 'driving school', naming it, rather presumptuously, the British School of Motoring. But he was very successful. Now known simply as BSM, it is the largest driving school in Britain. Developments in the United States began around the same time. However, the world's first ever driving school was founded much earlier, in 1898, in Paris. The Paris cab company, the Compagnie Generale des Voitures, set up their 'école d'apprentissage' in the Aubervilliers suburb of Paris as the very first school in the world to teach safe driving. The vehicles used at the school were electric urban taxis. The school had a series of reconstructions of Parisian streets, complete with cardboard cut-outs of pedestrians, cyclists, mother with prams, etc. In a report in the *Wide World Magazine*, a reporter visited the school and witnessed many 'pedestrians', 'cyclists' and 'mothers with prams' being mown down and 'killed', although fortunately only cardboard was damaged. The school's proprietor, M. Gourdon, reassured the reporter that after two weeks' training the apprentices would be able to safely negotiate Paris in their heavy electric taxis without mishap. However, the reporter said: 'I could not help wondering whether the familiarity of bowling over dummies did not tend to induce contempt for real human life.' The report contains a number of photographs which, in spite of poor quality, are worth reproducing here.

1898 Driving School in Paris

1898 Driving School in Paris

1898: THE FIRST DRIVER FATALITY

The first driver fatality is believed to have taken place in 1898 in the UK. Englishman Henry Lindfield and his son were driving from Brighton to London when, near the end of their trip, Lindfield lost control of his car whilst going down a hill. The car crashed through a fence and Lindfield was thrown from the driver's seat before the car ran into a tree, and he caught his leg between the tree and the car. His son was not hurt and ran for help. At the hospital, surgeons found the leg was crushed below the knee and decided to amputate it. After the operation, Lindfield remained unconscious and died the following day. If only that had been the first and last driver death!

1898: THE FIRST HEADLIGHTS

The very earliest cars had no lights at all, as they were not driven in the dark. When headlights became needed, cars relied on acetylene or oil lamps, which were robust but rather dim. Although the incandescent light bulb had been invented by Joseph Swan in 1860 and perfected enough to

'go public' in 1878, it took some time for electric illumination to displace oil and acetylene on the motor car. The very first electric headlamp on a road vehicle is believed to date from 1898 when the Electric Vehicle Company used them on their electric carriages. These early electric lights had numerous problems. The filaments burned out very quickly, especially on rough roads where the brittle filaments could easily break. Extensive development paid off, and by 1908 carbon-based headlamp bulbs running off the battery became available. Initially, however, the new headlamp was only available as a high-priced aftermarket upgrade to pre-existing car owners. In 1912, Cadillac rolled out the first modern electric headlamp system which, compared to its predecessors, could be used even during rain or snow without the risk of getting burned and could be turned on and off from within the car (what a luxury!). By 1924 the first 'modern' headlight, with both high and low beams, was available and, in 1927, the first foot-operated dimmer switch was on offer.

Left: 1912 Cadillac (Sicnag CC 2.0 via Wikimedia Commons)

Right: 1900 Lohner Porsche hybrid

1898: THE FIRST HYBRID CAR

When 'hybrid cars' are mentioned we naturally think of vehicles like the Toyota Prius which, in many respects, did herald the arrival of the modern hybrid. Indeed, today most manufacturers have hybrids in their range of vehicles. But provided we define a hybrid as being a vehicle which combines an internal-combustion engine, a battery and electric motors, hybrids have been around since

the dawn of motoring. In 1898 Dr Ferdinand Porsche built the first ever car to combine an internal-combustion engine, batteries and electric motors. This was the Lohner Electric Chaise shown in the photograph. The car featured a petrol engine which powered a generator, which charged the batteries, which in turn fed four electric motors, these being an integral part of each wheel. This is similar to the design of the modern Chevrolet Volt, which also has a petrol engine to drive a generator charging the battery, the only difference being that, in the case of the Volt, the petrol engine only runs when the battery is getting low.

Modern hybrids embrace more advanced technology, including regenerative braking. However, even this is not a recent idea. Forever at the forefront of adventurous design, Fred Lanchester produced a prototype hybrid in 1927. This had a petrol engine, battery and electric motors, the motors being used for starting and reversing, and when extra power was needed to climb hills. However, this car also had a form of regeneration in that when travelling at speed using the petrol engine, the electric motor worked instead as a generator to charge the battery.

1898: THE FIRST INDEPENDENT FRONT SUSPENSION

Many sources state that the first independent front suspension (IFS) was on the 1922 Lancia Lambda. However, this is incorrect. IFS was first used twenty-four years earlier on the 1898 Decauville which had a 'sliding pillar' system. The photograph here actually shows a Wartburg, but this was in fact a Deauville made in Germany under licence. In a sliding-pillar system the front

1927 Lanchester hybrid (Elliot Brown CC 2.0 via Wikimedia Commons)

1907 Sizaire-Naudin

1898 Decauville (Softeis CC SA 3.0 via Wikimedia Commons)

wheels are attached to a collar which can slide up and down on a tubular pillar which is attached to the car's chassis, usually on an outrigger. The pillar also typically contains the suspension spring, and being tubular allows the collar to rotate, accommodating the steering. The Decauville design was copied by Sizaire-Naudin a few years later. The photograph of a 1907 Sizaire-Naudin

shows very clearly the sliding pillar set-up. This type of suspension virtually died out after the Second World War, although it was used by Lancia into the 1950s, by Nash on its 600 model from 1940–49, whilst Morgan continue to use it to this day.

1898: THE FIRST MODERN SPARKING PLUG

As with many inventions, it is difficult to really pin down one 'inventor' of the modern sparking plug, as many people were working on similar ideas around the same time. The credit for the very earliest sparking plug possibly belongs to the Belgian engineer Étienne Lenoir (1822–1900), who used an electric plug in his 1860 gas engine, generally recognised as being the first internal-combustion piston engine. Three new patents for spark plugs were filed in 1898, by Nikola Tesla, Robert Bosch and the highly inventive Frederick Richards Simms. However, it was only the invention of a magneto-based ignition system that really made the modern ignition system feasible. The first such magneto, the Simms-Bosch Ignition Magneto, was developed by both Simms and Bosch through their joint venture Compagnie des Magnetos Simms-Bosch. But it foundered in 1906 on personal differences between the partners. Simms started a separate company, the Simms Magneto Company Ltd, but he was not a very astute businessman and it closed in 1913, leaving the field open for Bosch.

Subsequent improvements to the spark plug were made by Albert Champion, a Frenchman who emigrated to the US to set up the Champion business, the British Lodge brothers and Irishman Kenelm Lee Guinness (KLG). All three businesses thrived and are still going today.

1899: THE FIRST MODERN BRAKES

The very earliest cars used simple 'spoon' brakes as had been used on horse-drawn coaches. The first 'modern' type of brake was a variation on the drum brake. The first, or amongst the firsts, to wrap a cable around a drum anchored to the vehicle's chassis, the basic idea of a drum brake, was Gottlieb Daimler in 1899. Willhelm Maybach, the designer of the first Mercedes, utilised rudimentary mechanical drum brakes in 1901. These were steel cables wrapped around the drums of the rear wheels and operated by a hand lever. Louis Renault is, however, the man credited with the 1902 invention of the modern drum brake, which would become the standard for cars for many years. In the drum brake, brake shoes, which expand within the drum, generate friction by rubbing against the inner surface of the brake drum, which is attached to the wheel.

1899: THE FIRST DRIVING TEST & LICENCES

The world's first mandatory national driving test was introduced in France in 1899. In 1900 the first British person to pass a driving test was Miss Vera Hedges Butler, but she had to travel to France to take her driving test since driver testing would not be established in the UK for another thirty years. She must have been very keen to pass a test of driving proficiency! Drivers and pedestrians in the UK had to wait for the publication of the first edition of The Highway Code in 1931 before road safety began to improve. A voluntary driving test was introduced in England in 1935. The test cost 37½d and the pass rate was 63 per cent. The first person to pass was called Mr Been (really!). There weren't any test centres, and examiners would meet candidates at a pre-arranged spot, like a park or railway station. The compulsory driving test was introduced on 1 June 1935, for all drivers who started driving on or after 1 April 1934. Anyone who drove in the UK before 1934 didn't have to take the test.

In the United States, regulations varied between states. In 1899, New York and Chicago were the first cities to require testing before being allowed to drive a motor vehicle. In 1901, New York became the first state to register vehicles, whilst in 1903 Missouri and Massachusettes pioneered the requirement of a licence to drive a car, although in the case of Missouri this did not require the formality of actually passing any test of competency! Age restrictions on driving first appeared in the States in 1909, when Pennsylvania set a minimum age of 18, whilst Connecticut set the age as 16 provided the driver was accompanied by someone who held a full licence. All US states required cars to have licence plates by 1918, but the requirement to actually possess a driving licence took a long time to become nationwide. By 1935 only thirty-nine states were issuing driving licences.

1899: THE FIRST PRIVATE & PUBLIC GARAGES

Public and private garages, or 'motor homes', started to appear in the last few years of the nineteenth century. It is difficult to identify the first private garage as they are, by their private nature, less well documented than public buildings. However, there were certainly private garages being built prior to 1900. One of the earliest 'motor houses' was built in Southport in England by a local doctor called Dr W. Barratt. This was a two-storey building in the same style as the house, with a ground-floor garage with a concrete floor, electric lighting, heating and even an engine pit. In later years this was converted into residential accommodation. This pioneering 'motor house' (the term 'garage' came much later) was featured in the October 1899 edition of *The Autocar*.

In Germany two very early private garages still survive. At the Villa Esche, the Automobil Remise – or 'automobile carriage house' – built in 1903 still stands; whilst in Landenburg, Karl Benz, the 'father' of the motor car, had a tower built for himself in 1910 in which the ground floor was a parking area for cars, and the first floor was a study.

Custom-built public garages started appearing at around the same time as private garages, and the first recorded public garage was built in 1898 in Chicago as the Electric Vehicle Company Garage. In England, the Crystal Palace Garage in south London was constructed in 1900. One year later the first public garage in Germany, the Grossgarage der Automuller, was built in Berlin-Wilmersdorf.

1899: THE FIRST POLICE CAR

The first police vehicle in the world wasn't a car as such, but an electric wagon. In 1899, the city of Akron, Ohio bought a battery-powered 'paddy wagon' from the Collins Buggy Company for $2,400. It came with a cage for prisoners, a stretcher, electric headlights and a gong. But it only had a range of 30 miles and a top speed of 16mph, and just a year after it was bought an angry mob pushed it into the Ohio Canal. The first police vehicles which were actually cars were two bought by London's Metropolitan Police in 1903. The US city of Michigan followed in 1909 when the Police Commissioner Frank Croul, thinking the motor car could be useful to the police, bought the city America's first police car, a Packard, from his own pocket as the city refused to pay for it.

Interestingly, traffic police predate the motor car by around 150 years. In London, road traffic began to increase rapidly in volume in the eighteenth century and with no real rules to define how travellers should behave on the road the Lord Mayor of London, in 1722, appointed three men to ensure that traffic kept to the left and did not stop on London Bridge. They were almost certainly the world's first 'traffic police'. Records don't show if they were as unpopular as modern police are for many motorists!

1899: THE FIRST SALOON CAR (SEDAN)

The very first cars were all fully open to the elements, and the driver and passengers had to wear the right clothes to protect themselves from the cold and rain. It wasn't until the very end of the nineteenth century that enclosed bodywork started to appear. The very first saloon car (sedan) was the 1899 Renault Voiturette Type B. This was a version of Louis Renault's very first production car, the Voiturette Type A but fitted with doors and a roof. The two-seater was powered by a De Dion Bouton single-cylinder

1899 Renault Voiturette 'saloon'

1899 Peugeot Type 27

engine. Renault went on to produce four-seater saloons or 'limousines' from around 1905. Very shortly after Renault, Peugeot launched the Type 27, closely resembling a horse-drawn brougham. The American term 'sedan' first appeared on the 1911 Speedwell manufactured by the Speedwell Motor Car Company of Dayton, Ohio. The word sedan is probably derived from the Italian 'sedia' or chair, itself derived from the Latin 'sedere' which means 'to sit'.

1899: THE FIRST TRANSVERSE ENGINE

It is popular to believe that the original Mini pioneered the transverse engine. Whilst the Mini certainly made the engine layout well known and popular on account of how it made amazingly efficient use of space, the first transverse-engined car actually appeared sixty years before Issigonis's iconic design. The first car with this engine layout was the Critchley Light Car made by the Daimler Motor Company in 1899. The car was built with the clear objective

1931 DKW F1

of finding a home for fifty unwanted 4hp engines sent to Coventry by Daimler in Germany. The car was well regarded and sold well but was not intended to extend Daimler's range of high-powered expensive motor cars. For this reason it was named after Daimler's works manager James S. Critchley, rather than being called a Daimler. The car was equipped with advanced features, including pneumatic tyres and wheel steering. The engine was mounted transversely, with the flywheel rotating in the direction of travel. The water-cooled engine drove the rear wheels through a belt transmission, the belt being tensioned by moving the engine forward or backward in the frame. The first successful volume production of cars with a transverse engine was the DKW F1, which first appeared in 1931. After the war, the layout was used by Saab, Borgward and Hansa, but it was in 1959 with the launch of the Mini that transverse engines really came of age. The transverse layout works best with compact engines, but this didn't stop Bugatti producing a Grand Prix car, the Type 251, in 1955 with a transverse straight-eight engine!

1899: THE FIRST CAR WINDOWS

The very first cars had no windscreen (windshield) or windows. They were entirely open to the elements. It was only when closed cars appeared that side and rear windows were needed. The first fully enclosed car was the 1899 Renault Voiturette Type B, which was a version of Louis Renault's very first production car, the Voiturette Type A, but fitted with doors and a roof. Both doors had windows. A photograph of this car is shown under '1899: The First Saloon Car'.

Twentieth-Century Firsts

1900: THE FIRST FLAT-4 AND FLAT 6 CAR

The award for first flat-4 and first flat-6 can go to the same car, which had both engines as options. The Wilson-Pilcher car was the brainchild of Major Walter Gordon Wilson, a mechanical engineer and inventor who is credited, along with Sir William Tritton, with the invention of the tank in the First World War. An Irishman, he studied Mechanical Sciences at Cambridge, gaining a first-class BA degree. Whilst at Cambridge he often acted as 'passenger mechanic' for the Hon. Charles Rolls, a fellow undergraduate. Originally interested in aero engines, he collaborated with Percy Sinclair Pilcher and the Hon. Adrian Verney-Cave to build flat-format engines for small aircraft. But following Pilcher's death in an accident in 1899,

Wilson abandoned aero engines and developed the flat engine design for cars. He launched the Wilson-Pilcher car in 1900, and this was offered with either a flat-4 (2,715 cc) or a flat-6 (4,072 cc) engine, the world's first. Each water-cooled cylinder was separate and slightly offset from its opposite neighbour. The car also featured a novel gearbox of epicyclic design giving four speeds, and a

1900 Wilson-Pilcher

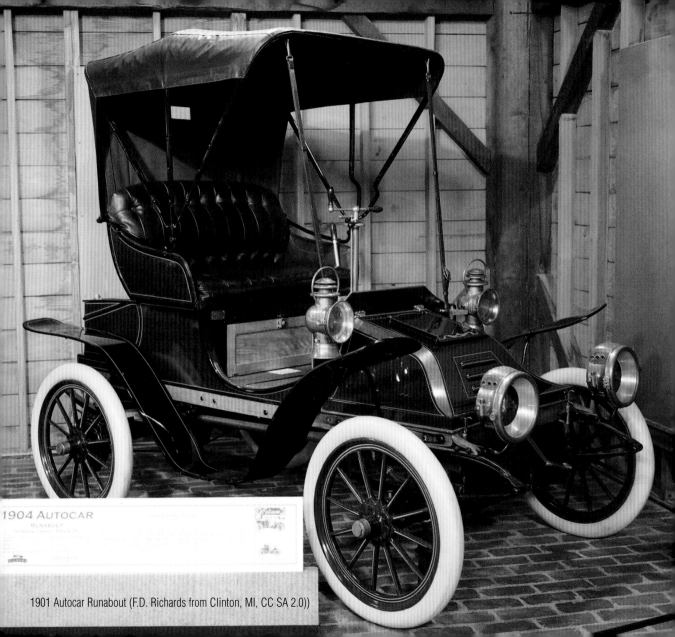

direct-drive top gear. In 1904 he joined Armstrong Whitworth who took over production of the car.

1901: THE FIRST MULTI-STOREY CAR PARK

The world's first multi-storey car park was opened in May 1901 by the City & Suburban Electric Carriage Company at No. 6 Denman Street in London. The Company specialised in the sale, storage, valeting and on-demand delivery of electric vehicles. These vehicles had a range of around 40 miles and could attain a speed of 20mph. The building had space for 100 vehicles over seven floors, and had a total floor area of 19,000sq. ft. The Company opened a second multi-storey in 1902 for 230 vehicles. No photographs appear to have survived of the 6 Denman Street Garage. The world's oldest surviving multi-storey car park is the Botanic Gardens Garage in Glasgow, built in 1907. Presumably because there was more space in most US cities than in London at the beginning of the twentieth century, America did not get its first multi-storey car park until 1918. This was built for the Hotel La Salle at 215 West Washington Street in the West Loop area of Chicago, Illinois.

1901: THE FIRST SHAFT DRIVE

The earliest cars were chain driven, that is the final drive from the differential gear to the rear wheels was by means of a chain rather than a solid shaft. It had great advantages in the early days by virtue of allowing a great deal of vertical movement of the driven axle, and it was simple and cheap to build. It also had less unsprung weight at the rear wheels. However, the superiority of shaft drive almost completely replaced chain drive, although Frazer Nash was a great fan of chain drive into the 1930s, using one chain for each gear selected by 'dog' clutches. The last chain-driven car was the Honda S600 of the 1960s. The first production car to feature shaft drive is believed to be the 1901 Autocar Runabout made by the Autocar Company, which was based in Hagerstown, Indiana. Autocar started making cars in 1900 with a single-cylinder chain-driven Runabout but switched to shaft drive for their 1901 model. Autocar ceased making cars in 1911 but continued manufacturing trucks.

1901: **THE FIRST TRAFFIC SIGNS**

The world's first traffic signs, that is signs aimed at directly informing road users, are almost certainly those erected in 1686 in one of the narrowest streets in Lisbon, Portugal. These signs stated which direction of traffic should have priority, and which should reverse back in case of congestion. One of these signs still exists in situ in Salvador Street in the Alfama district of the city, still serving its original purpose after over 300 years. The world's first 'modern' road signs appeared in the 1870s in Great Britain. These were designed to inform riders of high or 'ordinary' bicycles, otherwise known as 'penny farthings', of potential hazards ahead. They were erected by cycling organisations, and in particular the Bicycle Union, to give prior warning of hazards like steep hills, and thereby represented a significant step forward over signs which merely gave distances or directions to towns and villages.

The world's first road signs aimed specifically at motorists appeared in Gloucester, England in 1901, and by 1903 the British Government had introduced four 'national' signs based on shape. Signage adopted a more international approach when, at the International Toad Congress in Paris in 1908, nine European countries agreed on four basic pictorial symbols. In the United States, signs providing warnings or instructions for motorists started to appear in 1910.

1902: **THE FIRST ARMOURED CAR**

The larger-than-life Frederick Richard Simms (1863–1944) was an engineer, businessman, prolific inventor and motor-industry pioneer. He founded the RAC and the Society of Motor Manufacturers & Traders and introduced the words 'petrol' and 'motor car' to the English language. He also

1902 Simms Motor War Car

1899 Simms Motor Scout

designed the world's first armoured car, which was built for him by Vickers, Sons and Maxim at Barrow in Lancashire. The armoured car was based on a Daimler chassis. Simms had hoped to see his invention in action in the Boer War, but due to unforeseen production problems it was not finished until 1902, by which time the war was over. The vehicle was powered by a 3.3-litre, 16hp Cannstatt-Daimler engine, able to propel it at 9mph in spite of the weight of the 6mm armour. It carried two Maxim guns in a pair of rotatable turrets. At 28ft (8.5m) in length and 8ft (2.4m) wide, it was a large vehicle and was manned by a crew of four.

The world's first armoured car was revealed to the world at the Crystal Palace in April 1902. The first, rather poor-quality, photograph is one of the few which exist of this extraordinary beast. In spite of being extraordinary, it was an improvement on Simms' earlier military vehicle called the Motor Scout, which carried a gun and a petrol engine, but had minimal armour.

1902: THE FIRST DISC BRAKES

Today the vast majority of new cars have disc brakes, at least on the front wheels. They are much more effective than drum brakes, and less likely to 'fade'. Their superiority dramatically came to the public's attention in 1953 when a Jaguar C-type, fitted with disc brakes all round, stormed to victory at Le Mans mainly by virtue of being able to out-brake the Mercedes challengers at the end of the Mulsanne Straight. This set off a scramble by car manufacturers to fit disc brakes, especially to their upmarket models. Interestingly a BRM Type 15 had raced with Girling disc brakes two years earlier in 1951, the first use in Formula One.

Most people believe disc brakes started in the 1950s, but this is far from the truth. Development of disc brakes began in the 1890s in Britain, and a design for calliper-type automobile disc brakes was patented by Fred Lanchester in 1902 and fitted to his production cars from that year. Unfortunately the limited choice of metals at the time resulted in Lanchester having to use fairly soft material, with the result that the dust and stones from the rough roads at the time caused

Austin-Healey 100S (Herranderssvenson CC SA 3.0 via Wikimedia Commons)

1901 Lanchester with disc brakes (Clive Barker CC SA 2.0 via Wikimedia Commons)

them to wear extremely quickly. Lanchester soon reverted to drum brakes.

It was then a long time until discs appeared again on cars, although during the Second World War they were used on tanks and armoured cars. After the war the American Crossley Company launched its Crossley Hot Shot with Goodyear discs at the front, making it the first production car since the Lanchester so equipped. The first production car with discs on all four wheels was the 1953 Austin-Healey 100S, a high-performance version of the Healey of which only fifty were made. The first mass-production car fitted with discs was the Citroën DS which, from 1955 until the model ceased production twenty years later, had in-board discs at the front. Although Lanchester's design was flawed by the use of soft metal in his discs, his design looked and operated in a very similar way to modern disc brakes, so the 'first' must go to Fred Lanchester.

1902: FIRST AUTOMOBILE ASSEMBLY LINE

This may sound like automotive blasphemy! Henry Ford did not invent the automotive assembly line. Ford was only the third company to introduce this improved method of production. The honour of being first with a car production line lies with Ransom Olds, of Oldsmobile fame, and the credit for being second lies with Thomas B. Jeffery, an Englishman who emigrated to the States aged 18 and set up the original Rambler car company. Poor Henry has to make do with the bronze medal!

Olds set up the Olds Motor Vehicle Company in 1897, and in his first year sold just four cars. The business wasn't doing well when an investor called Sam Smith bought it and put Olds in charge again. In 1901 the factory burned down, and the only prototype saved from the fire was the Curved Dash Oldsmobile. By radically reducing the price, and making all parts interchangeable, the Curved Dash really took off and demand soon outstripped supply. This was when Olds introduced the idea of the production line, with defined repetitive operations and fixed stations for the assembly workers. By 1902 output reached 2,500 vehicles, increasing further to 5,000 by 1905. The car production line was born. Ford didn't introduce his production line until 1913.

1902: THE FIRST SHOCK ABSORBERS

Firstly, a short lesson in automotive engineering. The things we commonly call 'shock absorbers' are nothing of the sort. They don't absorb shocks, rather they dampen out longer-lasting up and down movements in a car's suspension that have been triggered by a bump or depression in the road. In the very earliest days of motoring, cars normally used leaf springs consisting of a number of 'leaves' tied together. As these springs move up and down the leaves rub together with a natural damping tendency. However, the degree of damping depends on numerous factors such as how wet the springs are. Ideally a separate damper is required. As coil springs became more popular the problem got worse, as coil springs have no such natural damping.

The first car manufacturer to incorporate dampers was Mors. Mors was an early French car

1902 Mors

pioneer who took part in motor racing as early as 1897 in the belief that racing was a good way to progress technology. Mors added pneumatic shock absorbers to their cars in 1902 which gave them a great advantage over the competition on the rough roads and racing circuits of the period. This was well demonstrated in their victory in the important Paris–Berlin race.

1902: THE FIRST SINGLE OVERHEAD CAM

The very first car with a single overhead camshaft was the 20hp Maudslay of 1902. The Maudslay Company was founded by Cyril Charles Maudslay to make marine engines. He was joined in the venture by his cousin Reginald Walter Maudslay, but Reginald soon left to set up his own company, the Standard Motor Company. The marine engines did not sell well, and in 1902 the Maudslays decided to make engines for automobiles instead. Their first engine, designed by Alexander Craig, was very advanced for its time, featuring the world's first overhead camshaft on a car engine, together with pressurised lubrication. The three-cylinder engine was followed in 1903 by a six-cylinder version, the first overhead-cam six to go into production. For 1904, a range of cars was on offer, including one with a 9.6-litre version of the six-cylinder engine. The cars were among the most expensive on the British market. The three-cylinder variant was also used in a novel petrol-powered railway locomotive for the London, Brighton and South Coast Railway to draw trucks to the meat market at Deptford. This was the first commercially successful petrol locomotive in the world.

1902 Maudslay

In the United States, just one year behind Maudslay, the Marr Auto Car Company introduced in 1903 the Marr, a two-seat 'runabout' with a single-cylinder, overhead-cam, 1.7-litre engine mounted under the seat. Unfortunately, the plant burnt to the ground in August 1904 with fourteen cars inside, and just one Marr Auto Car is known to exist today.

1902: FIRST V6-ENGINED CAR

The very first use of the V6 engine configuration was by Marmon, an American company which had started in 1851 manufacturing flour-grinding equipment. In the late nineteenth century they branched out into other areas of machinery, and in 1902 began limited car production. Their first model was a V-twin, which was soon followed by an air-cooled V4 and later V6 and V8s. Later they would switch to more conventional in-line engines. However, these early models were only made in very limited quantities. The first

1950 Lancia Aurelia B12 V6 (Threecharlie CC SA 3.0 via Wikimedia Commons)

mass-produced V6s came from Lancia with their Aurelia model in 1950, which lasted in production until 1958. Lancia had done a lot of research to find an engine that was compact enough to fit into limited bonnet space, yet which was also smooth, running and vibrationless. The research suggested a 60-degree V6 was the solution. In the 1950s the V6 configuration was something of a novelty, but today it is a popular format for both petrol and diesel engines, being cheaper to manufacture and more efficient than a similar capacity V8.

1903: THE FIRST FOUR-WHEEL BRAKING

In the early days of motoring the majority of cars only had brakes on the rear wheels. There was a near universal fear that brakes on the front wheels would result in cars skidding out of control. In reality, of course, most of the braking is fulfilled by the front brakes on a car since, upon braking, weight is transferred to the front wheels. The first installation of brakes on all four wheels was on the 1903 Spyker from the Netherlands, an extremely advanced car with permanent four-wheel drive and a powerful six-cylinder engine. The car still

1903 Spyker 60hp four-wheel drive (Alf van Beem CC 1.0 via Wikimedia Commons)

exists and is on display at the Louwman Museum in The Hague. Four-wheel braking took some time to catch on in the motor industry. A report published in 1929 stated that 70 per cent of British, US and Continental cars in Britain in 1924 were rear-braked only. However, as with many technological advances, once a few manufacturers started fitting four-wheel braking the rest quickly followed suit, and the report stated that by 1929 only 1 per cent of cars had only rear brakes.

1903: THE FIRST INDEPENDENT REAR SUSPENSION

The earliest independent-rear-suspension system on cars was the 'swing axle' type invented and patented in Germany in 1903 by the Austrian engineer Edmund Rumpler. This revolutionary invention allowed wheels to react to irregularities of road surfaces quite independently of each other, enabling the vehicle to maintain strong roadholding at all times. However, Rumpler did not apply his invention to a motor car until 1921 when he launched the revolutionary Rumpler Tropfenwagen. This car featured a 2,580cc (157cu. in.) overhead-valve 'W6' engine producing

36hp, with three banks of paired cylinders, all working on one common crankshaft. It was mounted just ahead of the rear axle. The engine, transmission and final drive were assembled together and installed as a unit. The rear axles were suspended by trailing leaf springs, while the front axle, a normal simple beam axle, was suspended by leading leaf springs. Able to seat four or five, all the passengers were carried between the axles, for maximum comfort, while the driver was alone at the front, to maximize his view.

1903: THE FIRST POWER-ASSISTED BRAKES

The first car to offer power-assisted brakes was the Tincher, a car produced from 1903 to 1908 in Chicago, Illinois. The car was named after its developer, Thomas Luther Tincher, but actually built by the Chicago Coach and Carriage Company using body sections and other components manufactured by the German Krupps steel works. The Tincher debuted at the 1903 Chicago Automobile Show, where its air-braking system was the technical wonder of the event. Not only could the air-system stop the car but it could also be used to inflate flat tyres and power the car's horn. The Tincher was also one of the costliest cars in production at the time, with a race version beginning at $12,000, equivalent in 2018 to a staggering $305,000. Custom coach work on the touring cars and coach models could raise the price even higher. Small Tinchers, riding on a 90in wheelbase, were priced in the $5,000–$10,000 range. However, well built as the cars were, demand was limited and the Tincher was discontinued in 1909 when the Company, and Thomas Tincher, both declared bankruptcy. The next power-assisted brake system to appear on a production car was in 1919, when Hispano Suiza launched a mechanical servo on its H6 model. Interestingly, mechanical servo brakes were used on Rolls-Royce and Bentley cars into the late 1950s.

1903: THE FIRST WINDSCREEN WIPERS

It appears as though at least four people thought up the idea of the windscreen wiper at almost exactly the same time. Whilst it is difficult to attribute the 'first' to any one of these, what is certain is that wipers were invented in 1903. The first designs have been credited to Josef Hofmann, a Polish concert pianist and inventor. However, at the same time Mills Munitions in Birmingham claim to have filed the first patent. Also in 1903, an American inventor, Mary Anderson, filed a patent for her 'window cleaning device' which was operated manually by a lever inside the vehicle, and this closely resembled the wipers fitted on many early cars. Three months before Anderson filed her patent Robert Douglass filed a patent for a 'locomotive cab window cleaner', locomotive being used in its broadest sense here and not confined to railways. Also in 1903, Irish-born Henry Apjohn patented an 'Apparatus for Cleaning Carriage, Motor Car and other Windows', which was stated to use either brushes or wipers and could be either motor or hand driven. It does look as though Apjohn can claim the first motor-driven wipers. Whatever, there can be no doubt that 1903 was the year of the windscreen wiper!

1903: THE FIRST PETROL-POWERED 4X4

The first four-wheel drive car driven directly from a petrol engine was the 1903 60hp Spyker specially built for the Paris to Madrid Race. It had permanent four-wheel drive and also featured four-wheel braking, another first back in 1903.

1904: THE FIRST ESTATE CAR/ STATION WAGON/SHOOTING BRAKE

Estate car, station wagon and shooting brake all mean essentially the same thing, the terms being used variously in different countries: a car-based vehicle which has the carrying capacity of a small van. In the States they became known as station

1903 60hp Spyker

wagons as originally they were depot 'hacks' working at and around railway stations. In Britain 'estate cars' were similarly 'hacks' working on country estates, whilst shooting brakes carried shooting parties and their guns and equipment, as well as the 'spoils' of the day in the field. The very first such vehicle was probably the 1904 Albion 24hp, which was available as a solid-tyred shooting brake. Albion had been founded in 1899 and produced their first car in 1900. Passenger-car production ceased in 1915, but in 1920 the Company announced that shooting brakes would once again become available. In the US, the Stoughton Wagon Company in Wisconsin began putting custom wagon bodies on Model T Ford chassis, and by 1929 Ford was by far America's leading producer of station wagons.

1904: THE FIRST HEMISPHERICAL COMBUSTION CHAMBER (HEMI-HEAD)

The word 'hemi-head' has become so linked to Chrysler that it is easy to fall into the trap of thinking Chrysler must have invented it. But they did not. Hemispherical combustion chambers were introduced on some of the earliest automotive engines, shortly after the concept of the internal-combustion engine proved itself viable for powering road vehicles. The name reflects the design of a domed cylinder head, which, with the top of the piston encloses a space that approximates a hemisphere. It is difficult to assign a clear 'first' here, but as early as 1903/4 two automobile makers were producing hemi-head engines. In Belgium the Pipe motor company in Brussels was developing hemi-heads in the late 1890s, showing their first car in 1900. However, some sources say the first Pipe with a hemi-head didn't appear until 1904. Interestingly, a very young Hans Ledwinka saw the engine in France and on his return to Bohemia designed a similar engine in 1905 which powered his Type S Nesseldorf, which would later become the first Tatra. Around the same time in the US, Alan R. Welch and his brothers, owners of the Welch Motor Car Company, were independently pioneering the hemispherical engine. Their power plant was a simple 20hp twin-cylinder engine with a single overhead camshaft. In 1910 General Motors bought the Welch business and discontinued the hemi-head. The Chrysler engines, known by the trademark 'Hemi', only appeared in 1951, with three

1904 Pipe

series of engines: the Firepower from 1951 to 1958, the second series from 1964 to 1971 and the latest starting in 2003.

1904: THE FIRST SPARE WHEEL

In the very early days of motoring there was no such thing as a 'spare wheel'. In the event of a puncture it was necessary to replace the inner tube with the wheel still on the car, a lengthy, tedious, often dirty and potentially dangerous task. Then, in 1904, the Stepney Combination Wheel appeared, making life for the pioneer motorists much easier. The inventors were Thomas Morris Davis and Walter Davies who had opened an ironmongers in Stepney Street Arcade and a small cycle and motor repair works at the rear of the Stepney Hotel. In 1904 the brothers patented the first practical motor-vehicle spare wheel. It was a spokeless wheel rim, mounted on which was a tyre of slightly larger than usual diameter. This rim and tyre could be attached to a wheel with a punctured tyre by adjustable clamps. Although it was only a 'get you home' accessory, like today's 'run flat tyres' and not suitable for extended use, it was widely adopted. The invention was

a great success and in 1906 they formed the Stepney Spare Motor Wheel Ltd, and opened the Stepney Wheel Works in Copperworks Road. By 1910 the company had international agencies throughout Europe and North America. After the First World War, the Stepney Wheel was displaced by replaceable road wheels but not before the Stepney wheel had made the two brothers very wealthy. The photograph shows a 1911 Rolls-Royce Silver Ghost with its Stepney Combination Wheel mounted just beside the driver's seat.

1905: THE FIRST 100MPH CAR

The first car to break the 100mph barrier was a 90hp Napier, a British car owned by Selwyn Francis Edge, an Australian-born businessman, racing driver and record breaker. In the early twentieth century rich 'petrol heads' like Edge would take their cars to Ormond Beach in Florida to play around with speed. In 1905, Edge's car, driven by Arthur MacDonald, achieved 104.65mph over a measured mile. However, his record stood for just fifteen minutes, because a twin-engined Mercedes then went faster, but this car was disqualified. So the crown for 'king of the ton' rests with MacDonald and Edge's Napier.

1911 Rolls-Royce Silver Ghost with Stepney Wheel (© Jörgens.mi/ CC BY-SA 3.0))

1905: THE FIRST AMPHIBIOUS CAR

Since the start of the twentieth century many people have tried to build a successful amphibious vehicle. Until the 1920s, attempts were very crude. Two solutions were tried. The first was to get a rolling chassis to float by fitting boat-like bodywork; the second was to simply fit a boat with wheels and axles ... and hope for the best! In 1905, one T. Richmond of Jessup, Iowa made a moderately successful craft. Like the earliest cars, this was also a three-wheeler with the single front wheel providing steerage both on the road and on the water. It was powered by a three-cylinder petrol engine, and when in the water propulsion was achieved by means of fins or paddles attached to the wheel spokes.

Amphicar (Mr.choppers CC 3.0 via Wikimedia Commons)

The boat-like hull was in fact one of the very earliest types of monocoque. There has only ever been one commercially successful amphibious car, which was the German Amphicar with almost 4,000 built between 1961 and 1968, many of which survive today.

1905: THE FIRST V8-ENGINED CAR

Although the V8 engine is traditionally associated with the American market, the very first V8-engined car was actually a Rolls-Royce, which pre-dated the first mass-produced V8s from Cadillac by ten years. Launched in 1905 it was designed to compete with the electric cars which were popular in towns and cities at the time. To achieve this it would have to be very smooth, very quiet and smokeless; power was seen as a secondary consideration. The engine was mounted at the front under the car to give the appearance of a town brougham, and so had to be very shallow. The solution lay in a 90-degree V8 configuration of 3,535cc. Two bodyshells were planned: a Landaulet Par

Excellence, to compete with the electric cars, and a more conventional-looking Legalimit. The latter was capable of around 26mph, but the engine was governed so as not to exceed the legal limit of 20mph, hence the vehicle's name. Although it is believed three were built only one was actually sold, to Sir Alfred Harmsworth, 1st Viscount Northcliffe the newspaper tycoon. The others were used as works cars for visiting customers. Although not a success, the V8 provided valuable

1905 Rolls-Royce V8 Landaulet

1905 Rolls-Royce Legalimit V8

experience for the Company, which went on to produce extremely refined six-cylinder models before eventually returning to the V8 format with the Silver Cloud II in 1959.

1906: THE FIRST REAR-VIEW MIRROR

It is not clear who invented the rear-view mirror for cars, nor when this occurred. An interesting reference is made to the use of a mirror in Dorothy Levitt's 1909 book *The Woman and the Car*. She wrote that women should 'carry a little hand mirror in a convenient place when driving' so they may 'hold the mirror aloft from time to time in order to see behind while driving in traffic'. Given the dim view today of people using a mobile phone whilst driving, I suspect an equally dim view would apply to drivers holding hand mirrors above their heads!

There are, however, competing claims. A trade magazine from 1906 alludes to the widespread use of mirrors in cars three years earlier, whilst Henri Cain of Paris patented a 'warning mirror' for automobiles in 1906. In 1908 the Argus Dash mirror was being advertised as allowing adjustment to see any part of the road behind. The first appearance of a rear-view mirror on the racing circuit was in the 1911 Indianapolis 500 when Ray Harroun installed one on his Marmon racer. However, he did admit it was useless because on the rough track it vibrated so much he couldn't see anything!

1906: THE FIRST SLEEVE-VALVE CAR ENGINE

The sleeve-valve engine was the invention of the American Charles Yale Knight (1868–1940). However, Knight could gain little interest in his invention in his home country, and all the early development of sleeve-valve engines was done in Britain. Irritated by the noise of poppet valves, Knight designed an engine where the valves became sliding sleeves within the cylinder. He was able to show a completed four-cylinder 40hp Silent Knight touring car at the 1906 Chicago Auto Show. But there was little interest from the car industry. One company, Pierce-Arrow, did put his ideas to the test and found that the sleeve valve did have advantages: over 30mph they found the design not only quieter but also more powerful and faster.

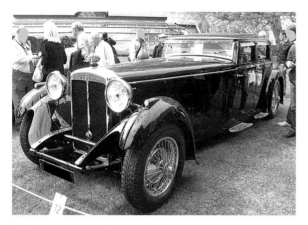

1932 Daimler Double Six

and the Empire, and 60 per cent of the rights in Europe, the remaining 40 per cent being taken by Minerva.

However, the sleeve valve would not last. The poor quality of lubricating oil at the time led to many engine failures, and the sleeve valve slowly died out. Sleeve valves continued for longer in the air, the impressive Napier Sabre aero engine being both very powerful and reliable. The photograph shows a 1932 Daimler Double Six, probably the most impressive car with a sleeve-valve engine.

However, as they considered speeds much over 30mph 'dangerous' the trial went no further. Pierce-Arrow also found the oil consumption very high, a well-known problem with early sleeve-valve engines. In despair, Knight travelled to England and managed to interest Daimler in his ideas. The fact that one of Daimler's directors was a fellow American might have helped a little! Daimler set up an undercover team to test and develop the sleeve-valve concept. The concept was developed so effectively that, once revealed to the industry, several European manufacturers became interested. Daimler purchased the rights to the design from Knight for use in England

1907: THE FIRST ROUNDABOUT

To many non-British people, the roundabout seems a very British thing and they probably assume it was invented in the UK. It is true that the world's oldest existing roundabout is in England in Letchworth Garden City, where it was placed in 1909. This survives to this day almost unchanged, albeit it is rather busier than in 1909.

Circular junctions have existed for a very long time, in such places as the Circle in Bath in England, the 1899 Brautwiesenplatz in Görlitz in Germany, and the Place de l'Étoile in Paris. However, these were not really roundabouts as

1909 Roundabout in Letchworth, UK

1907: THE FIRST WIRE WHEEL & FIRST TRUE 'SPARE' WHEEL

In the very early days of motoring there was no such thing as a 'spare wheel'. In the event of a puncture it was necessary to replace the inner tube with the wheel still on the car. Then in 1904 the Stepney Combination Wheel appeared (*see* separate '1904' entry), making life for the pioneer motorists much easier. But in 1907 the Rudge Whitworth Cycle Company introduced a much more satisfactory solution, the 'knock off' wire wheel. Whitworth had been founded by Charles Pugh and his two sons, Charles Vernon and John. In the early 1900s John put his mind to finding a better way of dealing with a punctured tyre than having to repair the tyre still attached to the car. In competition with Victor Riley of the Riley Cycle Co. they both developed a detachable wheel locked in place by a single large nut. Pugh took out a patent in 1908, but there were legal wrangles over the intellectual property rights to the design, and eventually Pugh lost out to Riley. One of the key features of the Pugh design is that it was self-tightening. The wheels on the right side of the car have a left-hand thread on the nut and vice versa. If the wheel becomes loose, the tendency is

we understand them, rather just circular roads. The first roundabout in the modern sense was probably the one built in 1907 in Hanchett Residence Park in San Jose, California. However, roundabouts would always be much more popular in the UK than in the States.

Widespread use of the modern roundabout system really began in the UK when the Government's Transport Research Laboratory (TRL) redesigned circular intersections during the 1960s. The TRL led the development of the offside priority rule and later invented the mini-roundabout to overcome safety and capacity limitations.

for the locking nut to tighten and hold the wheel securely. The system was taken up enthusiastically by the racing fraternity where the advantage of a quick-change wheel was obvious. For example, at the 1908 Isle of Man TT race, twenty-one of the thirty-five entrants used Rudge-Whitworth wheels, and only one of the finishers didn't. By 1913, the use of detachable wire wheels was universal in Grand Prix. The Rudge-Whitworth wheels therefore represented the first real 'spare wheel'.

1908: THE FIRST TRAFFICATORS

To most young people today, trafficators are as about as alien as the hand signals which used to be part of the driving test. Indeed many may never have even seen a trafficator!

Trafficators were the first type of automated turn indicators, and were semaphore signals which, when operated, protruded from a slot in the bodywork, either on the left or the right side, to indicate the intended direction of turn. They first appeared in the 1900s when they were actuated either pneumatically or mechanically. The earliest ones were not illuminated. The first to include illumination, and hence the first complete system,

was invented by Alfredo Barrachini in Rome in 1908. However, his system was still cable operated, electric operation appearing in 1918 when the Naillik Motor Signal Company of Boston added a motor drive. Motor drive was in turn superseded by a linear solenoid system which worked much more quickly. The final complete system, combining solenoid drive and internal illumination, arrived in 1927 courtesy of Berlin-based Max Ruhl and Ernst Neuman. Trafficators were common on vehicles until the introduction of the flashing direction indicators. As ever-tightening legislation prescribed the need for the modern type of flashing signal, trafficators became increasingly rare in the 1950s. Many historic vehicles used on today's roads have had their trafficators supplemented or replaced with modern indicators to aid visibility and to meet legislative requirements. It is likely that this topic will mean almost nothing to anyone under the age of 50!

1909: THE FIRST AIR-SPRUNG SUSPENSION

The idea behind air suspension is to provide a constant, smooth ride often combined with self-levelling. An air spring can combine springing

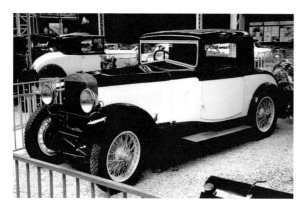

1922 Messier

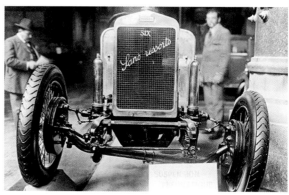

1922 Messier: detail of suspension

and shock absorbing into one unit, usually without the need for any metal spring. In the early days of motor cars, air suspension was not a great success. Ideas had been patented as early as 1901 by an American called William W. Humphreys, but he never made any practical units. The first air suspension to see production was in 1909. Some Crossley cars were fitted with a system developed by the Cowey Engineering Works Ltd of Kew in Surrey, UK. Although it was exhibited at the 8th International Motor Show at Olympia in 1909 and went into limited production, it was not a success as the system often developed leaks.

In 1920 a Frenchman by the name of George Messier began providing retro-fit air-suspension systems, and by 1922 he was producing his own Messier cars using his air system. A more significant development came in 1954 when Paul Mages, working in conjunction with Citroën, designed an air/oil hydropneumatic suspension which incorporated many of the features of the earlier designs. As a test bed Citroën replaced the conventional springs at the rear of a Traction Avant 15 with Mages' system in 1954, and it was deemed a success. In the following year Citroën launched the revolutionary DS with four-wheel, self-levelling, hydropneumatic suspension, and the DS has in many ways become the symbol of air suspension in passenger cars. It was the first car mass-produced with this type of suspension.

1909: THE FIRST CARPORT

The term 'carport' is derived from the French 'porte-cochère', which simply means a covered door. They were popular at country houses from the eighteenth century onwards, and they allowed passengers to alight from their coach under cover and enter the house without getting wet. By the time the car arrived on the scene very few new porte-cochères were being built, but those which already existed performed exactly the same function for car passengers who could alight before the chauffeur parked the car. The word carport is believed to have been first used by the American architect Frank Lloyd Wright in 1936 when he installed the first carport in the house he designed for Herbert Jacobs in Madison, Wisconsin. In describing the carport to Mr Jacobs, architect Wright said, 'A car is not a horse, and it doesn't need a barn.' He added, 'Cars are built well enough now so that they do not require elaborate shelter.' Looking back at life in 1936, it is easy to imagine cars prior to this time were not completely water tight and some shelter was essential. The carport was therefore a cheap and effective device for the protection of a car. Mr Jacobs added, 'our cheap second-hand car had stood out all winter at the curb, often in weather far below zero. A carport was a downright luxury for it.' However, carports were being built as early as 1909, when the architect Walter Burley Griffin installed one at the Sloane House in Elmhurst, Illinois and in 1913 the Minneapolis firm of Purcell, Feick & Elmslie included what they called an 'Auto Space' in the design for a house in Lockwood Lake, Wisconsin. Although carports did not become really popular in Britain until the 1970s, it is believed that the carport at Sutton Hoo, constructed in 1910, is the oldest surviving in the world.

1909: FIRST LAMINATED WINDSCREEN

Laminated glass has made a major contribution to safety on the road for well over 100 years. Before laminated glass, windscreens were either plain glass or toughened glass, either of which could shatter and cause serious injuries. Laminated glass was invented in 1903 by the French chemist Edouard Benedictus following an accident in his laboratory. A glass flask which had become coated inside with a film of the plastic cellulose nitrate fell off the work bench and shattered but did not break into pieces. However, it was not until 1909 that Benedictus filed a patent for his sandwich of glass and plastic. In 1911 he formed the Société du Verre Triplex (which literally means 'triple glass'), which started fabricating a laminated glass for motor cars. Production was complex and the material expensive, so it did not initially catch on in a big way. Later developments using different plastic cores, specifically polyvinyl butyral or ethylene-vinyl acetate (EVA), reduced the cost considerably, and gradually all countries started to require the fitting of safety glass in cars. The original company name of Triplex still lives on, the company now being part of Pilkingtons.

1910: THE FIRST ELECTRIC CAR HORNS

Warning horns date back to the earliest 'horseless' carriages. When steam carriages were beginning to become popular in the early 1800s, concerns started to mount about the safety of pedestrians. In 1865 a law was passed stating that 'self-propelled vehicles on public roads must be preceded by a man on foot waving a red flag and blowing a horn'. It soon became apparent that it would be much

more sensible to have the horn on the vehicle itself, operated by the driver. As the first motor cars appeared, speeds were low, and the simple bulb horn, where the driver squeezed the bulb, was seen as adequate. As speeds rose, a more sophisticated and louder horn was needed, and the breakthrough came with the invention of the first electric horn by Oliver Lucas in Birmingham, UK. His horn had a diaphragm which oscillated rapidly under the influence of an electromagnet which turned on and off many times a second, creating the sound.

1910: HYDRAULIC TAPPETS

Hydraulic tappets were popular on upmarket cars in the 1930s, such as the Rolls-Royce Phantom III and V16 Cadillac. They have the advantage of being quieter than simple tappets, and are also self-adjusting. Most sources claim that the 1930 V16 Cadillac was the first car to have them, but this is not correct. Hydraulic tappets are twenty years older than that. In 1910 a French car builder near Le Mans called Amédée Bollée invented the first self-adjusting hydraulic valve tappets. Bollée's two-piece tappets consisted of an upper and lower piston held slightly apart by a small spring. A port in the side of the lifter bore allowed oil to enter the cavity between the two pistons. Oil pressure pushed the upper piston up to remove slack between the tappet and valve. When the cam lobe raised the tappet, a one-way ball valve in the oil port prevented the oil between the pistons from leaking out. The oil trapped between the two pistons was incompressible, so the tappet acted like a solid member to push the valve open. However, hydraulic tappets have had until very recently a very chequered history, mainly due to unreliability, usually the result of poor oil quality. Although the Rolls-Royce Phantom III was equipped with hydraulic tappets in 1936–39, many were converted to solid tappets because of lubrication problems.

1912: THE FIRST FOUR-VALVE ENGINE

The first car featuring four valves per cylinder was the Ernest Henry-designed 1912 Peugeot L76 Grand Prix car, which was also the first car featuring twin overhead camshafts. Its 7.6-litre

1912 Peugeot Grand Prix Car (Agence Rol-Bibliotheque Nationale de France)

monobloc straight-4 with modern hemispherical combustion chambers produced 148bhp. In April 1913, on the Brooklands racetrack in England, a specially built L76 called 'la Torpille' (the torpedo) beat the world speed record of 170km/h. Also in 1913, Opel developed a single-overhead-cam engine with four valves per cylinder for its own Grand Prix car. This 4.5-litre vehicle produced 110bhp. Opel further developed the concept the following year, resulting in the most gigantic automobile the company has ever made, the

12.3-litre 'Opel Rennwagen', also known as 'Das Grüne Monster', the 'Green Monster'. The revised 12.3-litre four-valve engine developed a huge 260bhp, capable of propelling the 2,000kg monster to a maximum speed of 228km/h. Four valves per cylinder were only rarely seen in the 1920s, although the Bentley 3-litre was so equipped. They did not reappear until the late 1950s in motor racing, and it was via rallying that several manufacturers started using four valves again in the late 1970s and early 80s.

1912: THE FIRST MOTOR MUSEUM

The world's first motor museum was a short-lived enterprise, surviving for a mere two months in 1912. In 1899 Sir John McDonald, a founding member of the Scottish Automobile Club, made out a case in an article in the Automobile Club Journal for the creation of a British motor museum to record and preserve the history of the early stages in the development of the automobile. An initial approach was made to the Victoria & Albert Museum in London, but the Museum claimed they didn't have sufficient space. In 1909 the Imperial International Exhibition was held at London's White City and it included a small section recording the development of the car in the years leading up to 1901. Hoping to build on this, the Royal Automobile Club, as it was then known, approached the Science Museum in South Kensington hoping for a permanent exhibition devoted to the automobile. Again this was declined. In 1912 *The Motor* magazine, under the leadership of its owner Edmund Dangerfield, launched a new campaign to create a display of historic vehicles for the public to view. Within four months the trustees managed to assemble a collection of forty vehicles, and a temporary museum was opened on 31 May 1912 in the galleries of the Waring & Gillow store on Oxford Street in London. The exhibition was on two floors, the ground and first, plus a small exhibition area in the windows on Oxford Street. The oldest vehicle in the exhibition was the Crompton Steam Car, made in 1861. Others included early Panhards and Wolseleys, the J.H. Knight car, the first Argyll and an Albion. The display ran for just two months before it was placed in storage. It took eighteen months to find a new location, but in February 1914 it reopened at Crystal Palace in the building which had originally housed the Great Exhibition in 1851.

1912 Peugeot (Agence de presse Meurisse)

1912: THE FIRST DUAL OVERHEAD CAM ENGINE

Dual overhead cams have been a feature of high-performance engines for over 100 years. It is believed the first car powered by a twin-cam engine was the Peugeot built to compete in the French Grand Prix in 1912, which it won. Before 1912, racing cars had depended on very large, slow-revving engines for power and speed. The 1912 Peugeot was revolutionary in having four valves per cylinder and twin overhead camshafts, which permitted much higher engine speeds than most of its contemporaries. Success continued in 1913 with victories in the French Grand Prix and the Indianapolis 500 race.

The 1913 Indianapolis car would turn out to be highly significant in the history of American circuit racing. One of the racing Peugeots remained in the US when the First World War was declared. As parts could not be shipped over from France during the war, the car was looked after and repaired by Harry Miller who, at the time, had a young apprentice working for him with the name of Fred Offenhauser. Whilst at Miller the young Fred Offenhauser learned a lot from the design of the high-speed DOHC four-cylinder Peugeot engine, and in time this knowledge led to the design of the legendary Offenhauser 'four'. It is amazing to think the DNA of the Offenhauser engine derives from a 1913 Peugeot!

1913: THE FIRST UNITARY CONSTRUCTION

Unitary construction is where the body of the vehicle, its floorplan and chassis are a single structure made from shaped sheet steel, alloy or glass fibre welded or bonded together. This form of construction is much lighter and much stronger than the traditional separate chassis and bodywork. Today virtually all cars have unitary construction, although the separate chassis approach survived much longer in the United States than in Europe; the Lincoln Town Car maintained a separate chassis right through until 2011, whereas the last mass-produced car in the UK with a separate chassis, the Triumph Herald, was discontinued in 1971. The very first car with unitary construction on a production scale is often quoted as being the Lancia Lambda launched in 1922, of which

11,000 were made. However, this is not correct; the 1913 Lagonda 11.1 had a unitary structural body nine years earlier. The Citroën Traction Avant, launched in 1934, was the first very large-scale unitary-construction vehicle selling over 760,000 units over a twenty-three-year production period. Opel started unitary construction in 1935 with its Olympia and Kapitan models. Today unitary construction has become the industry norm.

1919 Filling station at Aldermaston (Automobile Association)

1913: THE FIRST DRIVE-IN PETROL (GAS) STATION

The world's first drive-in filling station opened to the public in Pittsburgh in 1913. Before this, car drivers simply pulled into almost any general or hardware store, or even blacksmith shops, to fill up their tanks from individual cans. The Pittsburgh filling station was a great success, selling on its first day 30 gallons of petrol; this may sound modest, but there were not many cars around in 1913! This petrol station was also the first purpose-built, architect-designed filling station, and it pioneered the distribution of free road maps.

The first drive-in filling station in England was opened in November 1919 at Aldermaston, Berkshire by the Automobile Association (AA). At the time, the AA was trying to promote the sale of British-made benzole fuel, a by-product of burning coal, as an alternative to imported Russian petrol. Prior to this, benzole from Russia had been widely available, but in the aftermath of the 1917 Russian Revolution, this trade was viewed in England as tantamount to supporting the Bolsheviks. At the Aldermaston filling station, with its single hand-operated pump, motorists were served by AA patrolmen in full uniform. The organisation opened another seven filling stations, and very soon the idea of selling British-made fuel took off, with 7,000 pumps in use by 1923. No photos of the Pittsburgh gas station survive, but the British one was captured on film.

1913: THE FIRST V12-ENGINED CAR

The first V12 installed in a car is believed to be the 9-litre (550cu. in.) engine used in the 1913 racing Sunbeam designed by chief engineer Louis Coatalen. This engine used four blocks of three cylinders each, arranged in pairs and in a 60-degree V with the inlet and exhaust valves operated from a single camshaft located within the V. An interesting feature of this engine was that there was no adjustment for the valves, every part having to be ground to the perfect size. This reflected Coatalen's desire to build aero engines based on the design. With aero engines, anything like valve adjusters, which can go wrong in the air, were to be avoided. The first V12 developed 200bhp at 2,400rpm and the car broke several records in 1913 and 1914. V12 engines enjoyed some popularity throughout the 1920s and 30s and are still sometimes seen today.

1913 V12 Sunbeam

1914: THE FIRST CAR WASH

The first car wash appeared in 1914 in Detroit, USA, when the 'Automated Laundry' opened. It wasn't really automated, however. The cars were pushed manually through a tunnel where one attendant would soap the car as it passed by, another would rinse and a third would do the drying. It was like an assembly line, but little more than a bucket and sponge job. In 1924 the Neway Auto Wash Bowl opened in Chicago by the Neway Auto Cleaning and Service Corporation. The approach here was different. The cars were first driven around in a pool of water to flush dirt and mud from the underside, and then driven up into a stall where the cars were washed in the normal manual way. The first 'automatic' conveyor car wash appeared in 1940 in Hollywood. This was a great step forward over the Detroit model as it pulled cars through by attaching a wire to the cars' front bumpers and winching them through. However, the washing and rinsing was still completely manual. Thomas Simpson is credited with inventing the first semi-automatic wash in 1946. This featured an overhead water sprinkler and three sets of manually operated brushes. The first fully automatic wash came in 1951 in Seattle courtesy of three brothers, Archie, Dean and Eldon Anderson. The Anderson clan's machine was completely hands-free; cars would be pulled through the tunnel and machines sprayed soap on them big brushes scrubbed them, nozzles rinsed them and giant blowers dried them. It proved a great success and became the model for the modern carwash. Needless to say, this was a big hit. Soon many other car-wash owners were installing automatic equipment in their businesses. Throughout the 1960s such machines spread across the States, and by the late '60s were appearing in Europe, Japan and many other countries.

1914: THE FIRST CENTRAL LOCKING

Today central locking is almost universal except on the very cheapest of cars. Modern systems also include features like boot (trunk) opening. Up until the 1950s, central locking of any sort was rare. It was first seen in a production car in 1914 on the very expensive Scripps-Booth. Packard introduced central locking as an option from 1956 onwards, after which it gradually became more popular on upmarket vehicles, before moving downmarket from the 1980s on.

1914: THE FIRST DESMODROMIC VALVES

The vast majority of cars have simple poppet valves, which are pushed open by a cam and then close under the pressure of a coil spring. In virtually all applications this system is entirely satisfactory. In the case of a desmodromic valve, both the opening and closing is done 'positively' by a cam, rather than relying just on a spring. This sort of fully controlled valve movement was conceived in the earliest days of car-engine development, and was mentioned in a patent dated 1896 but did not appear in any actual engine. Developing a desmodromic system which was reliable, not overly complex and economic took quite a long time. The first practical application was in a marine engine. Austin produced a 300bhp engine for a speedboat called *Irene I* in 1910. But this design did not find its way into any car engines.

The first car with desmodromic valves was the 1914 Grand Prix Delage. This revolutionary car had a 4.5-litre twin-cam twin-carburettor engine, but it proved unreliable and Delage did not continue with desmodromic valves. An Italian manufacturer, Azzariti, produced small 173cc and

114 GP Delage (Agence de Presse Meurisse)

348cc twin-cylinder engines with desmodromic valves between 1933 and 1934, but the company was short-lived. Desmodromic valves returned in the Mercedes-Benz W196 GP car in 1954 and 1955, and were also seen in the related 300SLR sports racing car of 1955. Maserati produced the 2,000cc four-cylinder OSCA Barchetta, also in 1955. Since then this valve system has not been used in cars. The photograph is of the 1914 Delage, and shows Louis Delage on the right.

1914: THE FIRST STREAMLINED CAR

1914 Streamlined Alfa 40/60hp (www.traumautoarchiv.de)

It is commonly believed that streamlined cars originated in the inter-war period of the 1920s and 1930s. The interwar period was a time of worldwide change. The 1925 Paris exhibition, officially titled 'Exposition Internationale des Arts Décoratifs et Industriels Modernes', marked the starting point of the Art Deco era. Influencing just about everything that had a design, the Art Deco movement began in Europe but soon spread to the US, expressed mainly through visual and ornamental arts such as architecture and industrial design. It didn't take long for the influence to impact on car design but in a modified form ... the Streamline Style. This was epitomised by cars like the Chrysler Streamline, the weird Dymaxion and the more sober early Tatras.

But streamlining predates the Art Deco period by over ten years. In 1914 Carrozzeria Castagna was commissioned by a certain Count Rocotti to fit streamlined coachwork to his Alfa 40/60. The standard Alfa 40/60 had a 6.1-litre four-cylinder engine producing 70bhp. In standard form it could achieve around 78mph. The Count's streamliner could do 86mph, an increase of nearly 10mph. There is a replica of this machine at the Alfa Romeo Museum. Production of the Alfa 40/60 was stopped in 1914 and resumed after the war, but the streamliner remained a one-off. The first production streamlined car was the Tatra 77 launched in 1934. This car, like most subsequent 'big' Tatras, featured a large air-cooled V8 engine at the rear which was very advanced for the time. The basic design continued, with much more modern bodywork, into the 1970s.

1934 Tatra 77 (joost j. Bakker CC 2.0 via Wikimedia Commons)

1915: THE FIRST RADIAL TYRES

Early radial tyres are usually associated with the name of Michelin, but whilst the French company certainly popularised this type of tyre from the late 1940s, they did not invent it. The first radial tyre dates back to 1915 when Arthur Savage, a tyre manufacturer and inventor in San Diego, filed a patent. Savage's patent expired in 1949. The first Michelin X tyre appeared in 1946, but there is no evidence that the Company knew about Savage's much earlier work. At the time Michelin owned the Citroën car maker, so it was a simple matter to bring the Michelin X tyre quickly into the market place. It appeared in 1948 on the Citroën 2CV. By 1952 the Company had developed a radial tyre for large commercial vehicles, definitely in this instance a 'first'. Because of the great advantages of the radial in terms of durability, handling and fuel economy, the technology spread very quickly across Europe and Asia. Initially the radial tyre faced resistance in the US because of reluctance by car makers to change suspension designs to take advantage of the new tyre format, and because the large tyre companies were also reluctant to retool their production lines. In any case, American roads didn't have many corners, unlike European roads, so road holding was not top of the agenda! It was not until 1970 that the first American car fitted with radials as standard appeared, this being the Lincoln Continental Mark III which bore Michelin radials. The first US tyre manufacturer to offer radials was Goodyear in 1974, the Company having been criticised for the heavy investment required. Sam Gibara, who headed up Goodyear between 1996 and 2003 claimed that the move into radials saved the company, which would otherwise have been taken over or closed down. Radials did nearly see the death of Firestone, however. In the mid-1970s Firestone decided to get into radials on the cheap, fabricating radial tyres on machines made for building bias tyres. Unfortunately, the tyres had a habit of disintegrating in a spectacular manner, and Firestone had to recall nearly 9 million of its Firestone 500 steel-belted radial tyres. Between 1977 and 1980 Firestone's tyre business dropped 25 per cent, resulting in the layoff of 25,000 workers. The company was only saved from death by being taken over by the Japanese tyre giant Bridgestone in 1988.

1918: THE FIRST ROAD MARKINGS

Many sources credit the first road markings to a certain June McCarroll who suggested the idea of a line down the centre of the road in 1924 in California. There is a competing claim by Edward Hines, who is supposed to have come up with the idea of a white line having been inspired by a leaking milk truck on a local street. However, there is no evidence of Hines' claim, and McCarroll's claim is six years after the world's first actual white line, which appeared in 1918 in the United Kingdom. The idea caught on very quickly and appeared nationwide, although their role in road safety was not really acknowledged until 1926.

1919: THE FIRST STRAIGHT EIGHT

Although the concept of a straight-eight car engine was conceived as early as 1903 by Charron, Girardot et Voigt, no straight-eight road car was produced before 1919. However, on the track there was a lot of work on straight-eight engines before the First World War, but these were mostly two four-cylinder engines joined in tandem. The first 'pure' straight eight, as opposed to twin tandem fours, is generally recognised as the Dufaux manufactured by C.H. Dufaux et Cie of Geneva. The aim was to enter the 1904 Gordon Bennett Race. The design was a 12,763cc (779cu. in.) side-valve with a bore of 125mm (4.9in) and a stroke of 130mm (5.1in) giving a bore/stroke ratio of a very high 96 per cent. It was claimed to produce around 120bhp at 1,300rpm, a very modest 9.4bhp per litre. Unfortunately, the car failed to start in either the 1904 or 1905 Gordon Bennett.

However, experience of straight eights for aircraft use in the First World War provided great strides forward in design for road use. The first road automobile with a straight-eight engine was the Isotta Fraschini Tipo 8 shown at the Paris Salon in 1919, whilst Leyland first presented their super-luxury OHC straight eight at the International Motor Exhibition at Olympia in 1920. In the US, Duesenberg were just one year behind, introducing their first production straight eight in 1921. Straight eights were used extensively by luxury car brands between the wars, including Daimler, Mercedes-Benz, Alfa Romeo, Packard, Marmon and Auburn. Interestingly, in Europe the straight eight

1919 Isotta Fraschini Tipo 8 (Alf van Beem CC 1.0 via Wikimedia Commons)

was used exclusively in very expensive upmarket vehicles, and were usually OHV and often OHC or DOHC, whereas in the US, development of a much cheaper flat-head straight eight saw it in much more middle-of-the-road offerings from the likes of Packard and Nash. The straight eight continued in just a handful of cars after the Second World War, including Daimler, Rolls-Royce, Packard and, of course, ZIL in the USSR.

1920s: THE FIRST DOOR LOCKS

It is not possible to identify which car actually had the first door locks, or when it happened. The earliest automobiles didn't have any security at all. It wasn't because there was no crime, it's simply because these cars were often owned by prestigious families who kept the vehicle in garages, or had someone on guard at all times. Some car makers had an ingenious idea, which was to have a detachable steering wheel, one that the owner could carry with him at all times. Then that person could leave his or her vehicle unattended while they went about their business. In fact, it wasn't until the 1920s, when car ownership was increasingly rapidly, that cars began to have lockable doors.

1920: THE FIRST (SAFE) CAR JACK

For the purposes of identifying a 'first' here, the car jack referred to is probably the first demonstrably safe car jack, rather than the first mechanism for raising a car. Some early jacks were simple vertical screws with a lug which engaged with a slot under the car. These could be very dangerous as the car could easily fall off the jack if the handbrake were not tightly engaged. The car jack is something which we will hopefully never have to use, but if we do have to use one, it is likely, today, to be a scissor jack which is almost universal. The scissor jack was invented and patented in 1920 by a Canadian named Joseph LaFrance. LaFrance's invention would look familiar to us today, as the design has scarcely changed over the last ninety-odd years. The jack had a base on which two legs, with 'knees' were attached, and the legs were separated at the 'knees' by a long screw operated by a detachable lever. When the lever was turned the screw reduced the distance between the 'knees' and the jack increased in height raising the car. Simple but ingenious at the time. The only significant development since 1920 has been the refinement made by Wilbur Jackson in 1949. This refinement in the design allowed the jack to be much more collapsible so it would easily fit discreetly in a car boot.

1920: THE FIRST WING MIRROR

It seems rather odd that we still refer to 'wing' mirrors when we consider that very few cars since the early 1970s have actually had mirrors on the wings. Today all cars have their 'wing' mirrors on the 'A' post, and with typically two electric motors and heating elements they contain nearly as much technology as a complete car back in 1910. It is believed that the first production car to feature wing mirrors was the Model T Ford in the early 1920s. For many years, only the driver's side had a mirror, and it was not until the 1940s that passenger-side mirrors appeared. The 1980s saw the appearance of mirrors which can be electronically adjusted from inside the car, and the 1990s the heated mirror.

1921: THE FIRST TORSION-BAR SUSPENSION

Torsion bars are rather like coil springs which have been straightened, and the spring action is created by twisting this bar. In fact the same twisting takes place in the coil spring although less obviously. Most of the credit for the wide acceptance of torsion-bar suspension goes to Dr Ferdinand Porsche who made it standard on most of his cars, beginning with the 1933 Volkswagen prototypes. By 1954 twenty-one makes of European car used torsion-bar suspension. However, Porsche was not the first to use torsion bars. The 'first' goes to the super-luxury 1921 Leyland Eight made in Britain, the most expensive British car on the market from 1921

1921 Leyland Eight

to 1923. The Leyland Eight had normal leaf springs at the front, but a mixture of leaf springs and torsion bars at the rear. At the rear the normal leaf springs were attached to the end of a transverse torsion bar, which allowed some rotation of the bush. The rear springs were therefore a sort of leaf/torsion-bar hybrid. At the front a form of torsion bar acted as an anti-roll bar by connecting the radius arms across the width of the vehicle. By way of contrast, in America only Chrysler went the torsion-bar route on its large-sized cars.

1921: THE FIRST CURVED WINDSCREEN

1921 Rumpler Tropfenwagen (Robotriot CC 3.0 via Wikimedia Commons)

Up until the Second World War, virtually all cars, even the most luxurious and expensive ones, had flat windscreens, sometimes split into a 'V' of two flat planes. After the war things started to change, and curved glass started becoming popular in the 1950s. It is popularly believed that this is when curved windscreens and windows first appeared. However, the curved windscreen is a lot older than most people think. The first car to have curved glass was the 1921 Rumpler Tropfenwagen. In fact all its windows were curved in order to aid streamlining. The Tropfenwagen was also notable for the first independent rear suspension.

1921: **THE FIRST FIVE-VALVE ENGINE**

The five-valve cylinder head is quite a rare configuration, usually having three inlet and two exhaust valves. With valves of similar size, this layout allows excellent breathing and high rpm. The earliest recorded five-valve engine dates from 1921 with Peugeot's triple-OHC five-valve Grand Prix car. In 1988 Audi built an experimental Quattro Turbo powered by a 2.2-litre turbocharged 25-valve straight-five, which produced 650bhp at 6,200rpm. It set two world records at Nardo in Italy, 1,000km (625 miles) at an average of 326.4km/h (202.8mph) and 500km (312.5 miles) at an average of 324.5km/h (201.6mph). Mitsubishi was the first to actually market a car with five valves per cylinder with their Minica Dangan ZZ in 1989.

1921: **THE FIRST HYDRAULIC BRAKES**

Although hydraulic brake systems did exist before 1921 they were not applied to production cars until that date. Fred Duesenberg was using hydraulic brakes on his racing cars as early as 1914, but he did not patent his ideas at the time and did not use them on his road cars. Malcolm Lockheed patented his system in 1917, but it would be four more years before they were applied to a production car. In 1921 a Lockheed-type system was fitted to all four wheels of one of Duesenberg's cars, a Model A. At first the system was plagued by problems of leakage because of the leather seals used, which dried out and shrank. Improvements came from the Maxwell Motor Corporation in the form of rubber seals. The system was available as an option on Maxwell-Chalmers cars from 1923 for $75. The first European car to have four-wheel

1989 Mitsubishi Minica Dangan ZZ

1921 Duesenberg Model A (Alf van Beem CC 1.0 via Wikimedia Commons)

hydraulic brakes was the British Triumph 13/35 model in 1924. During the 1930s hydraulic brakes became almost universal in most countries.

1921: THE FIRST SUPERCHARGED CAR

Although superchargers have been around since the 1840s it took a long time for them to be applied to cars. It is believed the very first supercharged car was a 'one-off' racing car built by Lee Chadwick of Pottstown, Pennsylvania in 1908 which reportedly could attain 100mph. However, it was not until 1921 that any production car would feature a supercharger. The first production cars fitted with superchargers were two Mercedes models, the 6/25 and the 10/40, which were shown at the Berlin Automobile Exhibition in 1921, sales beginning in 1923. The 2.6-litre engine of the 10/40 was retro-fitted with a supercharger, whereas the smaller 1.6-litre 6/25 was designed from the outset for supercharging. Interestingly, at the Exhibition, the models were described as 6/20 and 10/35, the more accurate designation of 6/25 and 10/40, reflecting the extra power over

the previous models, was not used until 1924. On both models the supercharger could be engaged and disengaged on the move. In fact, at the time continuous use of the supercharger was not recommended as it put too much of a strain on the engine. The two models were withdrawn in 1924, but Mercedes continued with supercharging albeit only on their larger models.

1923 Mercedes 6-25-40 (Michael Barera CC SA 4.0 via Wikimedia Commons)

1921 Rumpler Tropfenwagen

1921: THE FIRST 'W' FORMAT ENGINE

Today we are familiar with the W format engine in cars like Bentleys, with their VW/Audi-designed W12. The format is also found in the VW Phaeton and Audi 200, and also in the Bugatti with its W16 unit, and many believe these were the first incarnations of this complex engine design. But in fact the W-format car engine dates back to 1921. The 1921 Rumpler Tropfenwagen had a 2,580cc W6 OHV engine, the first engine of this format in a car. The photograph is the second one of this remarkable vehicle.

1922: THE FIRST CYLINDER DEACTIVATION

Cadillac became somewhat infamous for its highly unreliable L62 8-6-4 engines in 1981. The idea behind cylinder deactivation is that when an engine is less stressed, fuel economy may be boosted by closing down part of the engine until more power is again required. Many believe Cadillac pioneered this idea, but the concept is much older than 1981. The very first car to have this feature was the 1922 Wills Sainte-Claire A68 Roadster, with a 67hp V8. It had the ability to run on one bank of four cylinders if needed. It was a clever concept, but the Wills cars were just too

1921 Wills Sainte-Claire V8 A-68 Roadster

expensive to compete in the market. Renewed interest in the idea emerged during the Second World War, and experiments were carried out, but nothing reached production until 1981. That was the year Cadillac launched their L62 V8-6-4 engine across their entire range with the sole exception of their Seville, which used a 350cu. in. diesel. Both the 8-6-4 and the diesel unit ended up as failures. The diesel was simply a petrol V8 converted to diesel, so it lacked the strength to handle the much higher compression ratio and stress. The Eaton Corporation carried out further development work on the Cadillac engine, developing a control unit which could deactivate two or four cylinders when less power was needed. However, the engine proved very troublesome and was disliked by the traditional Cadillac buyers. A rash of unpredictable engine failures, and expensive warranty claims, led to the technology being quickly abandoned. After a long gap, car makers are beginning again to develop cylinder deactivation. Although the attempts to use variable-displacement technology failed in the past, automakers have been able to overcome the problems that occurred using new advancements in computers. With computers this fast cylinder deactivation and reactivation occur almost instantly.

1922: THE FIRST ONE-MAKE CAR CLUB

The first one-make car club is believed to be the Southern Jowett Car Club founded on 13 May 1922 in England. The following advert appeared in the Bradford Telegraph and Argus on 12 May 1922:

> Owners of Jowett Cars in the neighbourhood of Bradford are asked to meet at Manningham Park gates (main entrance) tomorrow, Saturday May 13th from 2.15 – 2.30. It is proposed to have a short run to Boroughbridge and after tea to hold a meeting to inaugurate a club restricted to the owners of Jowett cars

The Southern Jowett Car Club held its first rally on 26 August 1923. The Club's logo includes a 1923 Jowett Short Two that is still alive and well.

1922: THE FIRST CAR RADIO

Few topics highlight the difficulty of identifying the true 'first' more than that of the car radio. How should we define 'first'? Do we mean the very first time any sort of radio is reported to have been fitted in a car? Do we mean the first radio produced in serial volume which could be installed? Do we mean the first time a radio was offered as a standard option? Or perhaps the first radio fitted as standard equipment? There is no clear answer.

The very first radio of any sort installed in a vehicle was one fitted by Guglielmo Marconi in a Thorneycroft steam lorry in 1901. But this radio only received data not sound, and required a tall aerial to be erected whilst the vehicle was stationary. The first installation in a car is believed to be a modified domestic battery radio fitted to the passenger door of a Model T Ford by a high-school student named George Frost in Chicago in 1922. Also, the same year Marconi installed an eight-valve radio in a Daimler Light 20 limousine and it was displayed at the Olympia Motor Show that year. This had a large frame aerial on the roof. Also during the 1920s, a few motorists in Britain fitted a Marconi V2A cabinet radio to their car's running boards, whilst in the United States in 1922 it was possible to buy a Chevrolet fitted with a 'Westinghouse two-stage amplifying radio receiving set' for an extra $200, equivalent to around $3,000 today. In the UK, Daimler was also offering an optional radio with some of their top-range models. So credit for the first 'proper' car radio, installed as part of the original vehicle, must be shared by Daimler and Chevrolet. The credit for the first mass-produced radio must go to the American Galvin Manufacturing Corporation who, in 1930, were offering their Motorola brand radio for $130.

1922: THE FIRST REVERSING LIGHT

The first car to have a reversing light, or so-called 'back up light', was the 1922 Wills Sainte-Claire A-68 Roadster, the same car which first introduced cylinder deactivation.

1922: FIRST V4-ENGINED CAR

The Italian company Lancia was the first to manufacture a V4 engine. Indeed the company specialised in very narrow-angle V engines for many years. The advantage of the very narrow V, between 10 degrees and 20 degrees, is that both rows of cylinders can be housed in a block with a single cylinder head. The design also allowed a single camshaft to service both banks of cylinders.

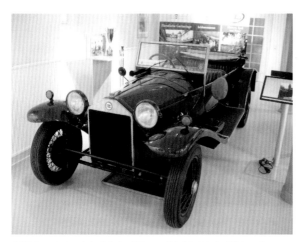

1922 Lancia Lambda (Michael Barera CC SA 4.0 via Wikimedia Commons)

The 1922 Lancia Lambda was the first car powered by this engine, and it continued in production until 1931. Its 49hp 2,119cc engine used a 20-degree V and a single camshaft. Interestingly the very narrow V engine has made a comeback in Volkswagen's high-performance V-engined Golfs.

1924: THE FIRST ALLOY WHEELS

Today, alloy wheels are all but ubiquitous and are used by automobile manufacturers as a key styling feature, often used to differentiate model ranges and equipment specification. They started becoming popular with the general public in the 1980s, and many believe that is when they started. Prior to the development of alloys, wheels were usually formed from two pieces of pressed steel, each half of the rim and disc, either welded or riveted into a single unit. Or, they were fabricated of a steel or aluminium rim, connected to a centre hub by metal spokes. A transitional design was a hybrid utilising a steel disc for strength and an aluminium rim for weight saving. Such a design was used by Porsche and Jaguar in the 1950s. Another example was the Borrani Bimetal, used on several Italian sporting models. Cast or forged alloy wheels offer reduced weight and greater stiffness than pressed-steel wheels. They also offer the designer almost unlimited freedom in terms of style. However, the alloy wheel actually dates from the 1920s. The use of cast-aluminium wheels was premiered by Ettore Bugatti on his Type 35 in 1924.

1924 Bugatti Type 35 (Dontpanic CC 3.0 via Wikimedia Commons)

These wheels incorporated an integrally cast brake drum. In addition to a considerable weight saving over a conventional wheel and separate brake drum, the Bugatti's wheels acted as large heat sinks to provide improved brake cooling. Bugatti continued development of cast wheels of this type, culminating in the massive 24in eight-lug version used on the Type 41 Royale.

1924: THE FIRST MOTORWAYS

It is a popular misconception that Germany's autobahns were the world's first motorways, that is highways dedicated to the high-speed travel of motor vehicles to the exclusion of bicycles, horses, pedestrians, etc., and with restricted access via special 'interchanges'. Although the autobahn network represented the first comprehensive system of such roads, and was planned as early as 1925, construction did not start until 1932 and was slow until Hitler came to power in 1933. Embracing the idea enthusiastically, by 1936 Hitler had 130,000 workers dedicated to the autobahn programme. It could be argued that the AVUS

'motor exercise road' built between 1913 and 1919 was the first purpose-built high speed road, but as it did not have any side-road access and could only be joined at the two termini, it was in reality just a race track, which it still is. The first roads we might recognise as 'motorways' were actually built not in Germany but in Italy. The very first of these motorways, the work of Piero Puricelli, was the Milano-Laghi road, connecting Milan with Varesse. It was planned in 1921 and completed between 1924 and 1926. The 42.6kmstretch still exists as part of the Autostrada dei Laghi. By the end of the 1930s Italy had over 400km of motorways, or 'autostrada', connecting cities and rural towns. The motorways were touted by Benito Mussolini in 1930 as one of the great achievements of his regime.

1926: THE FIRST CONSTANT VELOCITY JOINT (CVJ)

On cars with front engines and rear-wheel drive, the drive is taken to the wheels by the transmission shaft. Because the rear suspension moves up and down there must be flexibility in the transmission shaft. This is achieved using 'universal joints' invented by Gerolamo Cardano in the sixteenth century. However, the universal joint doesn't maintain a constant velocity as it rotates. In the case of the transmission shaft, the movements are small and the universal joint is entirely satisfactory. However, with a front-wheel-drive car, the movements of the drive shaft are much greater and the universal joint is unsatisfactory. Some 200 years before the car appeared, Hooke proposed the first constant velocity joint consisting of two Cardan joints offset by 90 degrees so as to cancel out the velocity variations. However, for use on front-wheel drive the double-cardan joint, whilst it would be satisfactory in function, is simply too long.

In terms of more practical CVJs there were two virtually simultaneous inventions which should perhaps share the 'crown'. Pierre Fenaille at Jean-Albert Grégoire's Tracta company filed a patent for the Tracta Joint in 1926; whilst in the United States, Alfred H. Rzeppa of the Ford Motor Company filed for a patent for the Rzeppa Joint. Both allowed smooth almost constant velocity to be transmitted at the sharp angles necessary for steering. The Tracta Joint works on the basis of a double 'tongue and groove' joint, and has only four individual moving parts, two forks and two slotted swivels. The two sections are, as

1929 Tracta (dave_7 CC SA 2.0 via Wikimedia Commons)

with Hooke's joint, 90 degrees apart to cancel speed fluctuations. The Rzeppa Joint uses two concentric shells with grooves into which a set of balls fit. With six balls and sets of grooves the drive is almost of constant velocity.

1928: THE FIRST PRE-SELECTOR GEARBOX

A pre-selector gearbox is one where the driver selects the next gear he will need, up or down, using a lever, and the gear is actually changed when required by pressing a foot pedal, which replaces the clutch pedal. This type of gearbox was invented by Major W.G. Wilson (1874–1957) who patented his design in 1928. Major Wilson interested Armstrong Siddeley in the idea, and a joint venture was formed under the name Improved Gears Ltd, later to change to Self-Changing Gears. Various manufacturers produced pre-selector transmissions under licence from Wilson. The Wilson gearbox was centred around a set of epicyclic gears engaged by a series of brakes, these being operated from a lever on the steering column. Pre-selector gearboxes disappeared around 1950, totally replaced by the fully automatic gearbox.

1928: THE FIRST SYNCHROMESH GEARBOX

Before the introduction of synchromesh, changing gear in a car would involve a double movement of the clutch pedal. When, say, changing up from second to third the gear lever would first be moved to neutral, the clutch pedal released momentarily before being depressed again and the gear lever moved into third. This was to make sure the shaft

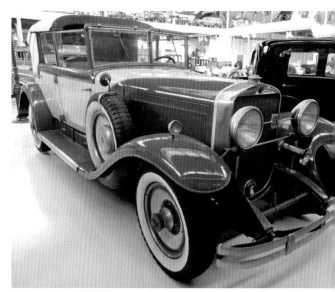

1928 Cadillac Type 341 (Sandra Fauconnier CC SA 3.0 via Wikimedia Commons)

in the gearbox was rotating at the correct speed to receive the selected gear. Synchromesh removed all that hassle. Syncromesh was invented by Earl A. Thompson who was born and raised in Oregon. He tested his invention on a range of vehicles and patented his idea in 1922 with US Patent 1,435,430. He travelled to Detroit to try to interest car makers in his invention. Cadillac liked his concept, and were quoted as saying that his invention 'for the first time enabled a driver to shift from low to second and from second to high or vice versa while the car is operating at any speed and without clashing of gears'. The device reached production in the 1928 Cadillac. Thompson was offered a job at Cadillac and eventually became assistant chief engineer, and went on to be instrumental in the development of automatic transmission.

1930: THE FIRST COMPULSORY CAR INSURANCE

Although the first car insurance policy is believed to have been taken out in 1897 in Ohio, it would be many years before any such insurance became compulsory anywhere around the globe. The world's first compulsory insurance for cars was introduced and enforced in the United Kingdom by the 1930 Road Traffic Act. Germany followed suit in 1939 with similar legislation.

1930: THE FIRST FOG LIGHT

By the 1930s cars had become significantly faster than in the previous decade, although speeds on roads outside towns still barely exceeded 40mph. As speeds increased so did a problem ... driving safely in fog, not least because few roads outside towns and cities had any form of street lighting or even good road markings. An innovation that Bosch patented in 1930 was to help with that. The earliest Bosch fog light was basically an additional headlight mounted low down on the bumper, and pointing downwards, which only illuminated a few metres in front of the car. It was assumed that under such conditions cars would be travelling very slowly, so the area requiring illumination was small. The engineers at Bosch realised that by mounting the light very low, the light would not be reflected back into the driver's eyes, which was the main problem with conventional headlights. From the mid 1930s fog lights were often fitted as a pair, giving a wide, low beam to left and right helping the driver locate the sides of the road. Today fog lights are still installed on cars but not in the prominent position of the 1930s.

1930: THE FIRST V16

The late 1920s and early 1930s saw a 'race for cylinders' amongst America's luxury car makers. Howard Marmon had begun work on what was intended to be the world's first V16 car in 1927, but he could not complete the production 'Sixteen' until 1931. Unfortunately for Howard, Cadillac had already introduced their V16 in 1930, so stealing the crown. To rub salt into Howard's wounds the Cadillac V16 has been designed by Owen Nacker, an ex-Marmon engineer. Peerless too were working on a V16 also designed by an ex-Marmon engineer, James Bohannon, which they would launch in 1932. The Cadillac Series 452 was the most exclusive model from Cadillac from 1930 to 1940. Up to 1937 the engine was a 7.4-litre (452cu. in.) OHV unit with a 45-degree V. In 1938 they changed to a 7.1-litre (431cu. in.) flat-head design with a 135-degree V, which allowed a lower bonnet line and was cheaper to make and service, yet delivered similar power to the OHV unit. However,

1930 Cadillac V16 (alijava CC SA 2.0 via Wikimedia Commons)

1931 Marmon V16 (Tino Rossini CC 2.0 via Wikimedia Commons)

it was never as popular or as well regarded as the earlier model. Although later being launched, the Marmon was technically superior, having an aluminium block with steel cylinder liners. Only 400 Marmon Sixteens were made before production ceased in 1933.

1932: THE FIRST LIMITED-SLIP DIFFERENTIAL

In a car with a simple differential, if one of the driven wheels looses adhesion on, say, a patch of ice, all the power will go to that wheel and it will spin at great speed, severely compromising the handling. A limited-slip differential is designed to allow a small degree of slippage before the differential 'locks' and returns power to both wheels. The first limited-slip differentials date from 1932 when Ferdinand Porsche designed the Auto Union Type C, an extremely powerful and fast rear-engined racing car. The car was so powerful that even at 100mph (160km/h) full throttle could induce severe wheel spin, especially when exiting corners. Porsche asked the automotive engineering firm ZF to design a differential which would limit the slippage and return full traction to both driven wheels. It was a great success and today is almost universal on very powerful cars.

1932 Auto Union Type C
(David Merrett CC 2.0 via
Wikimedia Commons)

1932: THE FIRST SPACE-FRAME CHASSIS

A space frame is like a cage built up from tubular sections onto which, in the case of a car, the mechanicals and the bodywork can be hung. It has the virtue of being extremely strong whilst light in weight. It is not the same as unitary construction, which virtually all cars have today; in unitary construction the strength is in the actual bodywork itself, whereas with a space frame all the strength is in the frame and the bodywork is just 'dressing'. The use of space frames in the automobile industry has always been very limited, but it does suit vehicles where the bodywork itself is not inherently strong, such as with fibreglass. It has, however, been extensively used in racing cars prior to carbon-fibre composite shells being used.

The first two automobiles with space-frame construction were both, to put it kindly, rather 'odd'. These were the Stout Scarab and the Dymaxion, two vehicles which rival each other for ugliness and weirdness! Both appeared at around the same time, 1932/33. The prototype Scarab appeared in 1932 and had a steel space frame clad with aluminium panels. The car looked a little like an art deco-style toaster, especially when the styling was updated in 1935 to include headlamps concealed behind a fine vertical-bar grille, and curved chrome trim linking the rear window to the bumper. In order to reduce costs the body panels were switched from aluminium to steel. Only nine Scarabs were completed, the main reason being that had it gone into serial production the price of the finished vehicle would have been prohibitive, around $5,000, or four times the cost of a Chrysler Imperial Airflow, and $100,000 in today's terms. The motorised art deco toaster is a rare beast indeed!

A rival for the first space frame, and a rival for the ugliest car of the period, was the 1933 Dymaxion. This was the brain child (or maybe brain

1932 Stout Scarab

1933 Dymaxion (Supermac1961 CC 2.0 via Wikimedia Commons)

nightmare!) of Buckminster Fuller. Just three were built. In fact it was never intended as 'just' a car, rather it was a design exercise for the terrestrial part of a flying car, one designed to fly, land and then drive with minimal disruption. The highly aerodynamic design was planned to give good fuel economy and high speed. The car had a rear-mounted V8 engine, and just three wheels, with the single rear wheel providing the steering. With this rear wheel being able to pivot around 180 degrees, the car could turn in its own length. As a car it was not a success. The handling was severely compromised at high speed or in any wind due to aerodynamic effects and the unnerving nature of its rear-wheel steering.

1932: THE FIRST SUN ROOF

These days most 'sunroofs' are what were originally referred to as 'moonroofs'. Sunroofs by historical definition are opaque, whereas moonroofs are transparent. The first opaque sunroofs were developed by the German company Webasto as an aftermarket installation from 1932 onwards. These were folding fabric sunroofs, and they were even fitted to full-size buses. The first car

company offering a sunroof as a standard option is thought to be Nash in the US who were offering the option on some of their 1937 models. The term 'moonroof', meaning a sliding sunroof featuring a glass panel, was coined in 1973 by the marketing team at Ford for the Lincoln Continental Mark IV. Initially these moonroofs were an aftermarket installation by the American Sunroof Company. Many moonroofs today also have a roller blind feature to make them opaque when the sun is strong.

1933: THE FIRST CAR AIR CONDITIONING

The earliest air conditioners in cars were not fitted as original equipment, but rather as aftermarket installations. In 1933 a company in New York was offering retro-fit air con, mainly to limousine companies rather than private individuals. The first car manufacturer to offer air conditioning as an original feature was Packard in 1939. However, the air-con unit was not fitted at the Packard factory. Instead, cars ordered with this device were shipped from Packard's factory to Bishop & Babcock in Cleveland, Ohio where the installation

Packard 180 (Rex Gray CC 2.0 via Wikimedia Commons)

was completed. The car would then be delivered to the local Packard dealer where the customer would take delivery. However, this conversion was not a big success, because the unit was very expensive and extremely bulky, and it had no temperature control; it was either on or off. It was also not very reliable, the long pipes going from the boot (trunk) where the compressor was located were prone to leaking. The air-conditioner option was discontinued in 1941. After the war, and after a long break, Cadillac and Packard began experimenting with new systems, but it was Chrysler in 1953 who first offered air con as an option on their Imperial model. Their Air Temp system was much more advanced than its rivals, having temperature settings of low, medium and high and very discreet ducting. From late 1953 Buick, Cadillac and Oldsmobile offered Frigidaire air-conditioning units across their ranges.

1933: THE FIRST CRASH BARRIERS

When motorways (freeways) were first constructed little need was seen to provide any barrier between the two directions of traffic apart from a simple central reservation. Crash barriers first appeared in the US in 1933, when steel barriers were offered by the Sheffield Steel Corporation of Kansas. The basic design has hardly changed since then. The one major change was replacing the originally painted crash barriers with the more modern galvanised ones, greatly extending the barrier's life by protecting it from corrosion. Crash barriers really rose to prominence after their introduction to the sport of Formula One, largely as a result of the Grand Prix Drivers Association's ongoing safety campaign in the late '60s and '70s. The barriers greatly reduced fatalities and serious injury on the racing circuits. Following their success in Formula One, barriers began to be added to motorways across the UK and Europe and parts of the United States.

1933: THE FIRST PRODUCTION CAR WITH A DIESEL ENGINE

Although the 'diesel' engine was invented as early as 1886 by Englishman Herbert Akroyd Stuart, it would take another forty-seven years before a diesel engine small enough and light enough to install in a car would appear. The first production 'diesel' car was the Citroën Rosalie in 1933, which featured a 1.8-litre diesel option in the Familiale, or estate car, model. The Mercedes-Benz 260D followed in 1936, and in the same year the Hanomag Rekord was launched. Many sources claim the Mercedes and the Hanomag were the first diesel cars; that is a myth! Citroën beat them by three years. The early diesel engines were very noisy and 'clattery' and not really suited to automobile use except in taxis, and it would take another forty years or so for diesel to be accepted in quality cars.

1946 Citroën hatchback

1934: **THE FIRST HATCHBACK**

We tend to think of the hatchback as a 1970s phenomenon, epitomised by cars like the VW Golf and Peugeot 206. But in reality the hatchback is much older, and dates back to the pre-war Citroën Traction Avant. This was launched on the market in 1934 as a 1.3-litre model called the 7A. Later, to expand the customer base, the car was made as an extended-length Familiale, or

family, model with three rows of seats capable of accommodating nine adults. The middle row could be folded away when not in use, making for cavernous rear legroom when configured with two rows. This stretched Traction Avant was also made as a 11 CV hatchback version, on which the tailgate could be raised to gain access to the passenger area, and just as on modern hatchbacks the rearmost seats could be folded flat to create a large luggage area. On this model, initially the tailgate was in two halves like the Range Rover, the lower of which folded down to form a platform, and carried the spare wheel. The upper opening cut into the roof level. When production resumed at the end of the war a one-piece top-hinged tailgate was introduced (as in the photograph). This car was marketed to grocers, butchers and tradesmen, and was the first true hatchback as we understand today.

1934: THE FIRST OVERDRIVE

An overdrive unit is a planetary gear which sits between the main gearbox and the final drive. It basically allows every gear to be doubled, so you may have first, overdrive first, second, overdrive second, third, overdrive third, and so on. Two companies dominated the overdrive market, Laycock de Normanville (British) and Borg-Warner (American). The Laycock system, developed by British engineer Edgar de Normanville, was operated by a switch, and so was completely under the driver's control, whereas the Borg-Warner system was semi-automatic and engaged when the throttle was reduced, and unengaged when the throttle was pressed again. In that sense the de Normanville system was a more 'pure' overdrive system. The Borg-Warner system was first seen in the 1934 Chrysler Airflow and DeSoto Airflow models. The de Normanville system first appeared on a production car in 1948 on the Standard Vanguard.

1934: FIRST REFLECTIVE ROAD STUDS

The first reflective road studs ('cat's eyes') appeared in 1934, the invention of a most remarkable Yorkshireman, Percy Shaw. He was born in Halifax into a very humble background, his father being a labourer at the local dye works. Percy grew up with three siblings and seven step-siblings and left school at 13. The family had moved to a very modest house in the Boothtown area of Halifax when Percy was young, and in spite of amassing enormous wealth he remained living in the same house until the day he died. He never married. His only apparent indulgence with his wealth was that he owned two Rolls-Royce Phantom Vs, one 'spare' for when the other was being serviced. The Rolls would be rather incongruously parked on the street outside his modest home, which was worth less than one of his cars! He never took a holiday and there was almost no furniture or carpets in his house.

His cat's eye design was a work of pure genius. It is said Percy was inspired by seeing the reflection of his headlights in cats' eyes at night. It was designed with a 'reservoir' below which would fill up with rainwater. Every time the stud was

1934: The first 'cats eyes'

1934: THE FIRST RUN-FLAT TYRE

Although 'run-flat' tyres can be driven on as an emergency 'get you home' facility, the main benefit of this sort of tyre is that in the event of a 'blow out' the tyre remains on the wheel rim, which adds greatly to safety allowing the driver to maintain control until he can stop. The first run-flat car tyre was developed by Michelin in France in 1934, based on experience with tyres for the Paris Metro and certain other commuter trains which ran on rubber tyres. The tyre had a safety rim inside the tyre which prevented the flat tyre from leaving the wheel rim. The tyre also had a special foam lining on which the rubber could 'ride'. Michelin claimed it was 'semi bullet proof' and well suited to military use and for armoured vehicles used by banks. However, the Michelin design was far too expensive for general use on ordinary cars.

driven over it would be forced downwards into the reservoir causing some of this water to be squirted onto the lenses, which would then be wiped clean by the rubber collar when the stud returned to its normal position. It was entirely self-cleaning and maintenance-free, a remarkable design. The reflective road stud was exported to most countries around the world, and has made a major contribution to road safety. Today cheaper road studs have been introduced, but none are as effective as Percy's original design.

The two main developments as far as private cars are concerned took place much later. In 1958 Chrysler and Goodyear collaborated to produce the 'Captive Air' run-flat tyres, which used a special interlining to carry the weight of the vehicle. Then in 1972 Dunlop launched the Total Mobility Tyre, later to be called 'Denovo', which first became optional equipment on the Rover P6 3500 in 1973.

By 1983 it had been further developed into the TD/Denloc tyre system, which was economical enough to be standard equipment across the entire Austin Metro range. Self-supporting run-flat tyres are now common on passenger cars and light commercial vehicles and typically provide for the vehicle to drive for 50 miles at around 50mph without risk of the tyre parting company with the wheel. However, these tyres carry a 20 per cent to 40 per cent weight penalty over similar standard tyres, and the thicker sidewall also means higher rolling resistance, which reduces the vehicle's fuel economy.

1935: THE FIRST PARKING METERS

We have the United States to 'thank' for the parking meter. Although a patent for a parking meter was filed as early as 1928, the design relied on the meter being powered from the parking car's battery. Needless to say the design got nowhere! Then in 1935, two engineering academics at the Oklahoma State University, Holger George Thuesen and Gerald Hale, at the request of Oklahoma City local government, designed the first practical meter which was known as 'the Black Maria', later to be called (more appropriately!) the Park-o-Meter. The world's first operational Park-o-Meter was installed by the Dual Parking Meter Company in Oklahoma City later in 1935. The meter was met with great indignation as Americans felt it was their right to park their cars wherever they wanted for free, and that the meters amounted to an unfair tax which had not been introduced by due legal process.

When first introduced, the meters charged 5 cents an hour, and were placed at 20ft intervals along the kerb, corresponding to spaces painted on the pavement. The parking meter caught on quickly and was loved by local shops, as they ensured a rapid turnover of parked cars, meaning more customers. By the early 1940s there were more than 140,000 parking meters operating in the United States. The idea took a long time to cross the Atlantic, and Britain was spared the parking meter until 1958.

1935: FIRST FOLDING METAL ROOF

The folding metal roof, or retractable hardtop, has become quite fashionable in recent years, and most manufacturers offer them. It is generally believed they are a recent innovation. But this is a myth! The concept is far from new, being over eighty years old. Although as early as 1919 Ben Ellerbeck in the US conceived the idea of a manually retractable hardtop on a Hudson coupe, it never saw production. The award for the 'first' must go to Peugeot who, in 1935, introduced a power-operated retractable hardtop on their 402 Eclipse Decapotable model, designed and patented by Georges Paulin. The French coachbuilder, Marcel Pourtout, also custom-built other examples of Paulin's designs on a larger Peugeot chassis. The first Eclipse 402s offered a power-retractable top, but in 1936 this was replaced by a more robust and reliable manually operated version on a stretched chassis, built in limited numbers until 1939.

1935 Peugeot Eclipse Decapotable

1935: FIRST TURBOCHARGED CAR

Probably the first car to be turbocharged was in 1935 when John Goddard installed a Bentley 8-litre engine in his 3-litre Bentley chassis, and added twin turbochargers, with sensational results. But this was a one-off. The first production car to be turbocharged was the Oldsmobile Jetfire released in 1962. The turbo was an optional extra over the basic cars, and significantly boosted the power from the 215cu. in. aluminium V8; incidentally this engine was virtually identical to the Buick engine which went on to power Rover and Range Rover vehicles.

The turbocharger used with this engine was a Garrett AiResearch unit.

Although the turbocharging gave a significant increase in power, the reliability of the turbo engine was poor and the Jetfire option was removed within just 12 months. An improved version of the turbo Jetfire engine was fitted to the Chevrolet Corvair Monza Spyder which was launched just one month later. In 1965 a turbocharged version of the International Harvester Scout was available, but again the model was short lived, being withdrawn in 1967. Over in Europe, 1973 saw the launch of the BMW 2002 Turbo, Europe's first mass-produced turbocharged car, but because of excessive turbo-lag, safety concerns and the oil crisis this was withdrawn within a year. At the height of the oil crisis, in 1974, Porsche launched the 911 Turbo, and turbos have remained part of the Porsche stable to this day. In 1977 came the launch of the Saab 99 Turbo, which was the first really successful turbocharged car, and in 1978 turbos were once again seen in the US in the form of the Buick Regal V6. Since the late 1970s turbos have really 'come of age' and all the early issues have been resolved.

Left: 1964 Chevrolet Corvair Monza Spyder (Joe Mabel CC SA 3.0 via Wikimedia Commons)

1935: THE FIRST WINDSCREEN WASHERS

Many sources claim the first windscreen washers appeared as an option on the 1937 Studebaker range. This is not true. The first car to offer windscreen washers as a standard production feature was the 1935 Triumph Gloria-Vitesse saloon. On this car the manually operated washers pointed downwards from the top of the windscreen. This had the advantage that in slow-moving traffic

1935 Triumph Gloria Vitesse (Mick CC 2.0 via Wikimedia Commons)

there was no risk of the jet spraying over the top of the car, missing the windscreen completely, nor at high speed the spray never getting above the scuttle. Both these problems are commonplace in modern scuttle-based installations. Interestingly on the Gloria Vitesse the fluid was drawn from the radiator header tank, so care was needed to make sure the engine water level didn't fall too low.

1936: THE FIRST BREATHALYSER

The idea of using a person's breath to test for alcohol levels in their body dates back to around 1874, before the automobile age. Today we use the word 'breathalyser' as a generic term for devices which assess alcohol levels in the blood from a sample of breath, but Breathalyser, just like other generic names like 'hoover', is actually a brand name, and it wasn't the first breath-testing machine. The first was the very aptly named 'Drunkometer' which appeared in 1936. Patented by Dr Rolla Harger, a professor of biochemistry and toxicology, the Drunkometer was a balloon-like device into which people would breathe to determine whether they were inebriated. In 1953, Robert Borkenstein, a former Indiana state police captain and university professor who had collaborated with Harger on the Drunkometer, invented the Breathalyser. This was much easier to use and more accurate than the Drunkometer, and so became the first practical scientific device available to police officers to establish whether someone had had too much to drink to drive. The suspect driver would blow into the Breathalyser and it would gauge the proportion of alcohol vapours in the exhaled breath. The result was indicated by a change of colour of some crystals. Today the Breathalyser, now digital rather than depending of colour changes, is only taken as a preliminary screening, the proper test being carried out at a police station on a much more sophisticated machine.

1936: THE FIRST CONCEALED (POP-UP) HEADLIGHTS

There appear to be two conflicting claims for the first concealed, or 'pop up', headlights. In 1936 both the Alfa Romeo 8C 2900A Pinin Farina Berlinetta and the Cord 810/812 had 'hidden' headlights, both cranked up manually one at a time from the dashboard. These headlights were mounted within

1936 Cord 810 (Sicnag CC 2.0 via Wikimedia Commons)

the front wings, which were aerodynamically smooth until the lights were cranked out. In the case of the Cord this feature became a 'signature' part of the design. Hidden headlights worked by electric motors were trialled by General Motors in 1938 and first appeared in a production model in 1942, on a DeSoto.

Electric and vacuum-operated systems continued to be used on a limited scale throughout the 1960s and 1970s, but some manual systems were still seen, such as that on the Saab Sonnett III, which used a lever-operated mechanical linkage to raise the headlamps into position. During the 1960s and 1970s many notable sports cars used this feature to comply with legal requirements about headlight height. Cars such as the Chevrolet Corvette, Ferrari Berlinetta Boxer and Lamborghini Countach could maintain very low bonnet lines so long as the headlights could be raised to the required legal height. However, since 2003, no modern volume-produced car used concealed headlights because they present difficulties in complying with pedestrian protection requirements.

1939: THE FIRST FLASHING TURN INDICATORS

According to an article published in the December 1985 issue of *Popular Mechanics*, the Protex Safety Signal Company designed a flashing turn indicator in 1920, although it appears no patent was filed at the time. The first patent seems to have been granted in 1925 to Edgar A. Walz, who tried to interest car manufacturers in his idea but with no success. His patent expired fourteen years later with no one showing interest. In 1939 Buick was the first manufacturer to offer factory-installed flashing indicators, as a 'safety feature'. It was marketed as the 'Flash-Way Directional Signal' and was operated from a switch on the steering column. At the time these flashing indicators were only at the rear of the car, but in 1940 Buick extended the flashers to the front of the car as well, and also added a self-cancelling feature. The same year they became standard on Buick, Cadillac and La Salle, and optional on Chevrolet, Oldsmobile, Pontiac, Hudson and Packard. Flashing indicators would not become popular in Europe until a long way after the Second World War.

1940 Buick Eight (John Lloyd)

1940: THE FIRST BUS LANE

Bus lanes are designed to speed up public transport by giving it dedicated lanes on a road. The world's first dedicated bus lane was introduced in 1940 in the city of Chicago, although the idea did not spread quickly. In Europe it would be twenty or so years before bus lanes appeared. Europe's first were created in Hamburg in Germany in 1963 at a time when the tram system was being shut down, and the area occupied by the tram rails could be dedicated to buses with little disturbance to the other traffic. This German project was studied by experts from many countries, including Japan, and similar systems started to appear around the globe. On January 1964, the first bus lane in France was introduced along the Quai du Louvre in Paris, whilst the first bus lane in London appeared in February 1968 on Vauxhall Bridge. What is believed to be the first contraflow bus lane was introduced in King's Road in Reading in the UK as a temporary measure when the road was made one-way in June 1968. The initial reason was to save the expense of rerouting the trolley buses which were due to be scrapped in November of that year. However, the experiment proved so successful that it was made permanent for use by motor buses, and is still in use today. By 1972 there were over 140km of bus lanes in 100 cities within OECD member countries, and the network grew substantially in the following decades.

1940: THE FIRST FUEL-INJECTED CAR

Many believe the first fuel-injected car engine was in the 1954 Mercedes-Benz 300SL. This is, of course, a myth. Fuel injection pre-dates its use in automobiles by over sixty years. Herbert Akroyd Stuart developed the first fuel injection similar to modern systems for his 'diesel' engines, using a 'jerk pump' to meter out the fuel oil at high pressure to an injector. Fuel injection with petrol engines started in aviation, and was in widespread use in the Second World War amongst German fighter planes. The very first application in a petrol-engined car was probably an experimental Alfa Romeo 6C 2500 which competed in the 1940 Mille Miglia. The engine had six electrically operated injectors fed by a semi-high-pressure circulating fuel pump system. The first production

1952 Goliath GP700
(Rewe CC SA 3.0 via
Wiikimedia Commons)

cars with fuel injection were the 1952 Goliath GP700 and the Gutbrod Superior, both introduced in 1952. These predate the 1954 Mercedes 300SL, which is often wrongly claimed as the first production car with fuel injection.

1940: THE FIRST GULL-WING CAR

It is popularly thought that the 1952 Mercedes-Benz 300SL pioneered the gull-wing door. Whilst the 300SL was indeed the first gull-wing car produced in any numbers, the very first gull-wing automobile appeared fourteen years earlier. This was the Bugatti Type 64 Coupe Atlantique. Jean Bugatti had planned and started to manufacture a limited run of three cars, but only one ever received coachwork before the designer's death road testing a Type 57. On a gull-wing car, the doors are hinged at the top rather than the side. In fact Bugatti referred to these doors as *'portes papillon'* or butterfly doors, but essentially they are exactly the same as gull-wings. After the 300SL there was a long gap until the next gull-wing doors appeared, most famously perhaps in the shape

of the DMC DeLorean from the 1980s. In total around eighteen different models have included gull-wing doors, including many 'supercars' like the Pagani Huayra, Bristol Fighter, Gumbert Apollo and Mercedes SLS AMG.

1945: THE FIRST CRUISE CONTROL/SPEED LIMITER

Cruise control is designed to keep a car at a constant speed. A speed limiter is designed to prevent a car going faster than a set speed. In some of the earliest cars a centrifugal governor effectively performed both functions. These governors were essentially the same as had been used on steam engines since James Watt and Matthew Boulton invented the idea in 1788. On the early cars the governor was necessary to prevent the engine being over-stressed. However, by setting different speeds on the governor, and then driving with his foot on the throttle, the driver effectively had cruise control. These were fitted to many cars up to around 1910, and no single 'first' can be identified. However, the first modern cruise control was invented in 1945 by Ralph Teetor. athoughit would be a number of years before

1958 Chrysler Imperial (Alf van Beem CC 1.0 via Wikimedia Commons)

1949 Aerocar (Chris857 CC SA 3.0 via Wikimedia Commons)

such a system appeared on a production car. The 1958 Chrysler Imperial was the first car to have a modern cruise controller fitted.

1946: THE FIRST FLYING CAR

In spite of many serious (and many more not-so-serious) attempts, there has yet to appear a viable flying car. In 1946 Robert Fulton's Airphibian appeared, which was basically just an aircraft adapted for travelling along the road. The wings and tail section could be removed for road travel, and the propeller accommodated inside the fuselage.

This was the first attempt at a flying car to be certified by the Federal Aviation Administration (FAA), so could lay claim to be 'first'. However, Fulton could not find a backer to allow him to continue development, so it came to nothing. In 1947 the ConvAirCar emerged from Consolidated Vultee, and was a two-door saloon with a detachable airplane unit. However, plans to market the car ended rather suddenly when it crashed on its third flight. Finally in 1949 we saw a viable machine, of which six were built. The Aerocar was built by Moulton Taylor and was designed to drive, fly and then drive again with minimum interruption. Taylor's car had a fibreglass shell similar to a light aircraft fuselage. A 3-metre-long drive shaft connected the engine to a pusher propeller. It cruised at 193km/h in the air and was the second and last roadworthy aircraft to receive FAA approval.

1947: THE FIRST ELECTRIC WINDOWS

Although powered windows, using a hydro-electric system, were available on various Ford Group and General Motors cars from 1947, the first pure electric power windows, as in modern cars, appeared on the top-of-the-range Daimler models in the UK, also in 1947. These models were the six-cylinder DE27 and straight-eight DE36. Power using just electric motors required these motors to be very small and light yet very powerful and they would need to fit easily inside the door itself, whereas the hydro-electric systems had a large hydraulic pump centrally with hydraulic pipes to each window. Chrysler introduced the first pure electric windows in the US four years later in 1951 with the Imperial model. General Motors followed in with full electric operation in 1954. Today electric windows are fitted even in the bottom-of-the-range cars.

1947 Daimler DE27 (PSParrot CC 2.0 via Wikimedia Commons)

1947: THE FIRST SELF-SERVICE PETROL (GAS) STATION

The world's first self-service petrol (gas) station is believed to have opened in 1947 by independent operator Frank Ulrich. He adopted the slogan 'Save five cents, serve yourself. Why pay more?' Although many were sceptical, his station was a resounding success, and he sold around a million gallons of petrol in the first week of operation. To add a spot of glamour, Ulrich had girls on roller skates going round collecting the money from customers. The idea did not catch on quickly, however, and many companies stuck with attendant service until the 1960s. Maybe there was a severe shortage of glamour girls who could roller skate! It was the arrival of remote access 'self-service', the current system, which changed everything. Many sources say the remote access station was the invention of John Roscoe in 1964. This is a myth. The world's first self-service petrol station with remote access opened in Plymouth in England in 1963. This was one year ahead of the US.

1949: THE FIRST GAS-TURBINE CAR

The very first car powered by a gas turbine, and therefore the first car with a rotary engine, was built by Rover in Solihull, England and completed in 1950. From the front it looked just like the sedate Rover cars of the period, but sedate is the last word anyone would use in reference to 'JET 1', the registration plate it carried and by which it would be generally known. It was a two-seat open car, with the jet engine positioned behind the seats. There were large air intakes on either

side, and the turbine exhaust was from the top of the 'boot' (trunk). It was a very fast car for 1950. Under initial tests it easily reached 88mph, and after further development it was speed trialled on the famous Jabbeke highway in Belgium, home to many speed trials, and achieved over 152mph. The technological achievement was seen as so significant that the Royal Automobile Club (RAC) awarded Rover the covered Dewar Trophy in 1951, a Trophy only occasionally awarded for outstanding achievement in the motor industry. JET 1 currently resides at the Science Museum in London.

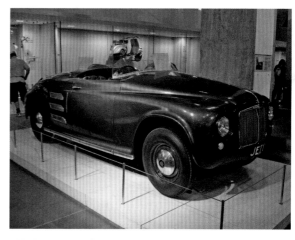

1949 Rover JET 1 (Oxyman CC SA 3.0 via Wikimedia Commons)

1950 Ford Zephyr (Sicnag CC 2.0 via Wikimedia Commons)

1950: THE FIRST MACPHERSON STRUTS

The increasing popularity of front-wheel drive in the 1970s and 1980s called for a more compact form of front suspension which would provide more room for the front drive axles. The MacPherson Strut, developed in the 1940s by Earle S. MacPherson at Chevrolet, offered a solution. This system combined the coil spring, hydraulic shock absorber, upper suspension arm and steering pivots in one unit. The prototype Chevrolet Cadet built in 1946 incorporated the first MacPherson struts, but the project was cancelled in 1947 and MacPherson left Chevrolet to join Ford. After joining Ford the first production cars to feature the struts were in the UK, the 1950 Ford Consul and Ford Zephyr. Ironically, these cars were not front-wheel drive, which the new suspension had been designed for. It is widely thought that the 1949 Ford Vedette in France pre-dates the British cars, but in fact the Vedette initially had wishbone suspension at the front, only changing to MacPherson struts in 1954 and then as the Simca Vedette, as the Ford factory had been taken over by Simca.

1951: FIRST POWER STEERING

Power steering was one invention which took a very long time to really catch on. As early as 1876 a certain G.W. Fitts received a patent for a power-steering mechanism, but very little is known of him or his work. In 1900 Robert E. Twyford was granted a patent for a four-wheel-drive system which included a mechanical power-steering mechanism. Then in 1902 the highly inventive

1951 Chrysler Imperial (order_242 CC SA 2.0 via Wikimedia Commons)

Frederick W. Lanchester patented a hydraulic power system in the UK. However, none of these ideas made it into production. It would not be until the 1920s that a successful power-steering system emerged, and not until the 1950s that a system was offered on a production car.

The big leap forward came when Francis W. Davis, an engineer in the truck division of Pierce Arrow, began exploring how steering could be made lighter. In 1926 he was able to demonstrate a practical system in operation. Davis then moved to General Motors and further refined his system, but GM decided it would be too expensive. The Second World War saw rapid development of power steering for heavy military vehicles, but it would not be until 1951 that a production car, the Chrysler Imperial, would be offered with a system based on some of Davis's expired patents.

1952: THE FIRST AUTOMATIC HEADLIGHT DIMMER (DIPPER)

In 1952 General Motors offered their Autronic Eye on their Oldsmobile and Cadillac models. This was the first automatic headlight dimmer (dipper). When a phototube mounted on the dashboard detected approaching headlights, it would automatically switch the car's beams to low until the other lane was clear. Despite reportedly being overly sensitive and unreliable, the Autronic Eye evolved, and versions spread to other GM brands and continued in Cadillacs until the 1988 model year. The Eye also made its way into GM's fantastic fleet of stylized Futurliners.

1953: THE FIRST SPEED HUMP

We have the Americans to 'thank' for the speed hump. Amazingly, this 'scourge on the motorist' was devised by a Nobel Prize winner, Arthur Holly Compton (no, his prize was not for inventing the speed hump! He was a physicist who worked on electro-magnetic theory). The Chancellor at Washington University in St Louis, Missouri, he was concerned about the speed of traffic passing Brookings Hall on the university campus and the danger to students and staff. So in 1953 he designed his 'traffic control bumps' to reduce speed. There is an earlier claim from 1907 when the *New York Times* reported on the use of raised pedestrian crossings to 'kill' speed in Chatham, New Jersey. According to a publication by the Institute of Transport

Engineers, the first speed bump in Europe was built in 1970 in the city of Delft in the Netherlands. Now we have them everywhere!

1954: HYDROPNEUMATIC SUSPENSION

Hydropneumatic suspension is a type of vehicle suspension which uses both fluid and gas to provide a sophisticated system offering self-levelling ride-height control and exceptional comfort, especially over rough surfaces. The fluid system allows the front and rear suspension units to 'communicate' through small hydraulic pipes rather than any mechanical device, affording great design flexibility. The system allows the height of the vehicle above the road to be adjusted on the move, something conventional suspension systems don't. It was invented and pioneered by Citroën, having been designed by Paul Magès. The system has been licensed to other manufacturers, notably Rolls-Royce for their Silver Shadow model, and to Mercedes where it's called 'Active Body Control'. It was during the Second World War that Paul Magès, an employee of Citroën with no formal

1970 Citroën SM (Ministry of Trust CC SA 4.0 via Wikimedia Commons))

Citroën DS (Oxfordian Kissuth CC SA 3.0 via Wikimedia Commons)

engineering training, developed the concept of an oil/air suspension system to offer self-levelling and super-soft ride. Although the system is most commonly linked to the Citroën DS, it was actually tested in 1954 on the rear suspension of a Traction Avant 15 using the hydraulic fluid used in braking systems. In 1954 the Citroën DS became the first production car to apply the technology, with the high-pressure hydraulic system also providing power steering, power brakes and gear changing. In 1965 Rolls-Royce took out a licence on the system for the Silver Shadow. In 1970 the Citroën system reached its peak of sophistication in the Maserati-powered SM model, which added speed-sensitive power steering to the mix.

1954: THE FIRST TUBELESS TYRES

The tubeless tyre had a long history before it first became available on a production car, the 1954 Packard Clipper. The very first patent on a tubeless tyre was granted in 1903 to P.W. Litchfield of the Goodyear Tire Company. However, this development was not commercially exploited due to their high cost. In 1918 a patent was granted to Frederick B. Cumpston for 'an improved tubeless pneumatic tire casing and improved rim and locking', but the tubeless tyre was still not a commercial success. In 1946 the B.F. Goodrich Company applied for a patent that 'relates to pneumatic tires and is advantageous especially where it is desired to use the tire without an inner tube'. The tyres underwent development and high-speed testing, were put into service on a fleet of taxis and were also used by some Ohio State police vehicles. The testing was successful, and in 1952 the patent was granted, at which point the Company began commercial development of the tyre, and by 1954 it was being offered on Packard's Clipper model, the first car to carry tubeless tyres.

1955: THE FIRST THERMOELECTRIC COOLING FAN

Today 85 per cent of the world's cars use thermoelectric engine-cooling fans. The thermoelectric fan was pioneered by Kenlowe, a company based in Maidenhead in England, and first launched in 1955. Prior to their introduction, cars had fans driven directly from the engine, so as long as the engine was running the fan was working. The purpose of the fan was to draw cooling air through the radiator, especially when the car was sitting in traffic. Of course, this was essential to prevent the engine overheating when the car was stationary, but when the car was moving the natural flow of air through the radiator was sufficient, and the fan was not required. The thermoelectric fan solved this problem as it is only activated when the temperature of the cooling water exceeds a preset level.

1955: THE FIRST CATALYTIC CONVERTERS

The first catalytic converter was developed by the French engineer Eugene Houdry around 1950, and was for use in smoke stacks. Houdry, an expert in catalytic oil refining, moved to the United States in 1930. When the report on the study of the Los Angeles smog was published, Houdry became concerned about the role played by the exhaust from both smoke stacks and automobiles. He founded a company called Oxy-Catalyst to develop and manufacture catalytic converters for smoke stacks, and then later for warehouse forklift

trucks which operated in confined spaces and ran on low-grade unleaded petrol. By the mid 1950s he started development of a catalytic converter for automobile engines. However, widespread use of catalytic converters in cars only started in the 1970s following regulations in most countries banning the use of tetraethyl lead as an 'anti knock' agent. The tetraethyl lead in petrol disables the converter by coating it with lead. The use of catalytic converters then spread rapidly from the US to most countries worldwide.

1955: THE FIRST FULLY ADJUSTABLE SEATS

In the early days of motoring, car seats were very basic, the only movement available being fore and aft to accommodate drivers of different heights. Every other element of the seats was designed for 'average' people. The first car to offer anything more was the 1955 Ford Thunderbird, which offered up-and-down adjustment as well as fore and aft. When power seats became available, much more adjustment started to be offered, and the need for 'seat adjustment memory' arose. Again, Ford came up with a solution. In 1957 Ford

1955 Ford Thunderbird (Morven CC 3.0 via Wikimedia Commons)

introduced their 'Dial-a-Matic' seat system in the Thunderbird and Mercury Cruiser models. Instead of plain switches, the Dial-a-Matic seat used a letter-and-numerical dial to adjust the seats fore/aft and up/down. When the ignition was switched off, the seat moved back to the rearmost, lowest position to allow easy exit and entry. When the car was started up again, the seat moved back to the last dialled position.

1958: THE FIRST STANDARD-FITMENT SEAT BELTS

Early car seat belts were simple lap belts, and were offered as options by Nash from 1949 and by Ford from 1955. The first car to have belts as a standard fitment was the Saab GT750 in 1958. Although a patent for a three-point belt was granted in the US in 1955 to Roger W. Griswold and Hugh DeHaven, the major credit for the first modern belt must go to two engineers working for Vattenfall, a Swedish power generating company owned by the Swedish Government. Fatal car accidents were increasing rapidly in Sweden in the 1950s, and when a study of accidents amongst Vattenfall employees revealed that the majority of casualties came from car accidents, Bengt Odelgard and Per-Olof Weman started to develop what would become the first modern three-point belt. The company and the two inventors gave their design to Volvo in the late 1950s, where it was improved by Nils Bohlin. Bohlin was able to confirm the effectiveness of the modern seat belt by analysing 28,000 accidents in Sweden. He found that unbelted occupants suffered fatal injuries at all speeds, whereas none of the belted occupants were fatally injured at speeds below 60mph provided the passenger compartment remained intact.

1958 Saab GT750 (Liftarn CC SA 3.0 via Wikimedia Commons)

1958: THE FIRST SPEED CAMERAS

There is a patent dating back to 1905 for a device with the rather sinister title of 'Time Recording Camera for Trapping Motorists'. The purpose of this device was clear, although it is not known if any were made. However, the origin of the speed camera we know today is much more benevolent! A Dutch rally driver by the name of Maurice Gatsonides wanted to monitor his speed on a race track in a better way than having someone use a stopwatch over a measured distance. So he designed and built the first speed camera, which became known as the Gatsometer. Setting up a company called Gatsometer BV, he started supplying his cameras to police forces to catch speeding motorists. The early Gatsometers used photographic film, and at speeding 'hotspots' would quickly run out of film. Gatsometer BV produced the first 'red light' camera in 1965, and the first portable speed camera in 1982. The introduction of digital technology and the use of a network connection to a central location greatly improved the effectiveness of the speed camera and avoided the need for someone to change the photographic film. We may curse at the speed camera, but it was a great concept which has probably saved many lives.

Gatso Camera (Andrew Dunn CC SA 2.0 via Wikimedia Commons)

1958: THE FIRST CONTINOUSLY VARIABLE TRANSMISSION (CVT)

Continuously variable transmission (CVT) has a surprisingly long history. The first patent for a CVT system was taken out in 1886 in Europe, and the first car to actually incorporate a rudimentary CVT was a Clyno car in 1923. However, this was an experimental model which never made it to market. CVT made better inroads in motorcycles, with Zenith Motorcycles in 1910 offering a V-twin-engined bike with the Gradua-Gear system. This Zenith-Gradua was so successful in

hill-climb events, it was barred to give other manufacturers a chance! Then in 1912 the British manufacturer Rudge-Whitworth built the Rudge Multigear, which used an improved version of the Gradua-Gear system. However, in the car market the real crown should go to the Dutch company DAF who successfully launched the DAF 600 Daffodil in 1958 using the van Doornes CVT system under the name Variomatic. An intruiging feature of the DAF 600 was that, as it had no gears, when switched to reverse mode it could go as quickly backwards as forwards. With its 590cc flat-twin engine it wasn't fast, but could just about reach 70mph ... forward and reverse!

1958 DAF Daffodil

1962: THE FIRST CHILD SAFETY SEAT

Since the first car was manufactured and put on the market in the late nineteenth century, many modifications and adjustments have been implemented to protect those that drive and ride in motorised vehicles. Most restraints were put into place to protect adults without regard for young children. Though child seats were beginning to be manufactured in the early 1930s, their purpose was not the safety of children. The purpose was to act as booster seats to bring the child to a height easier for the driving parent to see them. It was not until 1962 that two designs with the purpose of protecting a child were developed independently. British inventor Jean Ames created a rear-facing child seat with a Y-shaped strap similar to today's models: American Leonard Rivkin, of Denver Colorado, designed a forward-facing seat with a metal frame to protect the child.

1964: THE FIRST INTERMITTENT WINDSCREEN WIPERS

Taken for granted today, the 'birth' of the intermittent windscreen wiper was quite a painful one for some and involved one of the most protracted, expensive and bitterly fought court cases in the history of the motor car. The concept was designed and developed by an American inventor by the name of Robert William Kearns. Kearns was granted a patent on his idea in December 1964. Recognising its great value in light rain or mist, he sought to interest the three large US car manufacturers in his idea, but his overtures came to nothing. However, having seen

the technology, all three manufacturers developed their own similar systems and began offering the feature on their cars from 1969. Kearns took Ford and Chrysler to court for patent infringement, and won both cases. He received $10.1 million in damages from Ford and $18.7 million from Chrysler. With costs the total settlement was around $85 million. Maybe small fry for Ford and Chrysler, but a very satisfactory outcome for Kearns. Since 1969 intermittent wipers have been a feature on virtually all new cars.

1964: THE FIRST ROTARY CAR ENGINE

Let's start with exploding a myth. The Wankel engine is NOT a rotary engine. In a rotary engine the centre of gravity of the moving parts remains on the same axis. In the Wankel engine the rotor 'wobbles' or oscillates inside the complicated-shaped combustion chamber, hence it's an oscillating engine not a rotary engine. Although the Rover JET 1 was the first-turbine powered car, the only car to have reached any

1964 Chrysler Turbine Car (Lebubu93 CC SA 3.0 via Wikimedia Commons)

degree of 'production' with a rotary engine was the Chrysler Turbine Car, of which fifty-five were built between September 1964 and January 1966 for public trial. At the end of the trial all were recalled by Chrysler and most were scrapped. However, Chrysler kept two, five are in museums, and two are in private collections.

1965: VARIABLE SPEED LIMITS

The first known experiments with variable speed limits took place in Germany in 1965 on a 30km stretch of the A8 Autobahn between Munich and Salzburg across the border into Austria. The mechanically changed signs could display limits of 60, 80 or 100km/h, as well as text signs for 'accident' and 'danger zone'. Traffic was monitored by video and the signs changed manually as required. Later in the 1960s, busy sections of the New Jersey Turnpike were equipped with variable speed signs as well as messaging signs. In Britain it was not until 1995 that variable limits appeared, firstly on the busy section of the M25 between Junctions 10 and 16. Modern variable-speed-limit systems can operate without manual intervention, sensing traffic flows and road conditions automatically and adjusting the speed signs accordingly.

1966: THE FIRST ANTI-LOCK (OR ADVANCED) BRAKING SYSTEM

The idea of anti-lock brakes dates back to the late 1920s and early 1930s. The German engineer Karl Wessel patented a system in 1928, but he never built a prototype. Robert Bosch also patented a fairly similar system in 1936, but again Bosch never actually manufactured a working prototype. It would take another twenty years for any practical system to emerge, in the shape of the Dunlop Maxaret Anti-Skid System. At first this was used in the aviation industry where it achieved remarkable results, reducing braking distances by around 30 per cent in wet or icy conditions. Tyre life was also extended.

On the road the first application was an experimental trial on a motor cycle, but although it was extremely successful the company did not see a future for the technology on two wheels. The first use in a car was on the Fergusson P99 racing car in the 1960s. The first road car to have anti-lock brakes was the Jensen FF (a development of the Interceptor) which was produced between 1966 and 1971. A total of 320 were made. There was also an experimental four-wheel-drive Ford Zodiac equipped with the same system. Electronically controlled anti-lock systems were developed in the late 1960s, replacing the earlier mechanical system. Electronic systems were used on Concorde.

1966: THE FIRST HEATED SEATS

This is another example where 'first' requires some interpretation. The first patent for heated seats appeared in the early 1950s, filed by Robert Ballard of General Motors, but nothing further happened for a number of years. It is understood that the first car fitted with heated seats as an optional extra was the 1966 Cadillac Fleetwood, whilst the first standard fitting was on the 1972 Saab 99, 95 and 96 models. The Saab press release announced:

> The electrically heated driver's seat, standard in the Saab 99, 95 and 96 models, is another exclusive Saab feature for 1972. Built into the seat pad and backrest of the seat, the system heats up automatically and quickly when the ignition is turned on and the interior temperature is below

1966 Jensen FF (Brian Snelson CC 2.0 via Wikimedia Commons)

58°F. A thermostat turns off the heat when the seat temperature reaches 82°F. The heating system is completely safe from electric shock and is not affected by dampness or water that might come in contact with it

As a contemporary source added, the 'not affected by dampness' implies it is safe to wet your pants in your Saab!

1967: THE FIRST MARKED BOX JUNCTION

When we think of a box junction we normally think of the hatched yellow area in the centre of the intersection which you shouldn't enter unless your exit is clear. However, in many countries, the concept of the box junction exists even if it is not marked. In the US, apart from in a few areas including New York and Colorado, no special road markings are used to indicate this rule, but some governments post warning signs to increase awareness of the law at problematic intersections. The first marked box junctions appeared in 1967 in the UK following a successful trial in London.

1968: THE FIRST AIRBAGS

Rudimentary patents for airbags date back to the 1950s. However, the airbag industry really started in 1968 when a New Jersey mechanical engineer named Allen K. Breed invented a reliable inexpensive crash sensor. His crash-sensing technology is considered the world's first electromechanical automotive airbag system. Earlier compressed-air systems were replaced by an explosive charge, and the risk of injury from the bags themselves was reduced by designing bags which inflate within milliseconds and immediately

1973 Oldsmobile Toronado (Illegitimate Barrister CC SA 3.0 via Wikimedia Commons)

begin to deflate, providing a soft cushioning effect. Airbag development was focused on the US partly because seat-belt wearing in the early 1970s was relatively low by international standards. The first production car for sale to the public equipped with airbags was the 1973 Oldsmobile Toronado.

1968: THE FIRST HEAD RESTRAINTS

Head restraints, often wrongly referred to as head rests, are an automotive safety feature attached to, or integral with, the seat to prevent or at least limit rearward movement of the occupant's head relative to their torso in order to minimise the risk of whiplash or injury to the cervical vertebrae. Although patents for head restraints were filed as early as 1921 by a Benjamin Katz in Oakland, California, and other patents appeared in 1930 and 1950, none of these initiatives appear to have resulted in restraints being included in new car design. The first cars to be sold with effective restraints were Volvos in 1968. This was quickly followed by other manufacturers and, in 1969 in the US, the National Highway Traffic Safety Administration mandated that all new cars sold in the States must have head restraints which met Federal standards.

1968: SEAT BELT LAW

It would appear that the first law relating to seat belts took effect in 1968 with the federal law 'Title 49 of the United States Code, Chapter 301, Motor Vehicle Safety Standard'. However, this only required seat belts to be fitted to all vehicles except buses, and did not require the belts to be actually worn. The very first law requiring belts to be worn was put in place in 1970 in the State of Victoria in Australia. This legislation was enacted after a trial with Hemco seatbelts, designed by Desmond Hemphill (1926–2001), in the front seats of police vehicles. This significantly lowered the incidence of injury and death amongst the police force. In the UK, compulsory seat-belt wearing became law in 1983, whilst in the US, New York was the first state to enforce compulsory belt wearing in 1984.

1974: THE FIRST IN-LINE FIVE-CYLINDER ENGINE

The history of the in-line five-cylinder engine goes back to the 1930s. Ford developed an inline-five in the late 1930s for a small economy car design, but this never saw production. There was little demand at the time for small cars in the US. In the 1930s Gardner made a straight-five 7-litre diesel, the 5LW, for use in buses and boats, but a straight-five engine did not see production for passenger cars until Mercedes-Benz introduced the diesel W115 3-litre diesel model in 1974. The first production petrol straight-five was the 2.1-litre T5 introduced by the Volkswagen Group in the Audi 100 range towards the end of the 1970s. The same engine was used in the famous Quattro rally cars. In-line 'fives' became popular for use in mid-range brands where manufacturers wished to expand their model range without going for a full six-cylinder option. In recent years this engine format has fallen out of favour.

1976: THE FIRST AUTOMATIC NUMBER PLATE RECOGNITION (ANPR)

Automatic Number Plate Recognition (ANPR) has revolutionised many aspects of policing on the roads. The ability to automatically read number plates, even at great distances, and automatically link the information collected to police and government databases enables the highway police to check almost instantly whether cars are taxed and insured, even when they are travelling at great speed. The first ANPR system was developed in 1976 at the Police Scientific Development Branch in the UK. Prototypes were working in 1979, and contracts to produce ANPR machines in quantity were awarded initially to EMI Electronics, and then later to Computer Recognition Systems (CRS) Ltd in Wokingham, UK. Initial trials of the system were undertaken at the Dartford Tunnel and on the A1 road north of London. Interestingly, the first arrest arising from ANPR technology was in 1981 as a result of identifying a stolen car. Widespread use of ANPR, especially in police cars, really started in the 1990s as cheaper and easier-to-use systems became available. ANPR systems are now also used to collect data for solving possible future crimes as well as active incidents. No system today is 100 per cent accurate, of course, and in the UK an accuracy of 97.5 per cent is accepted ... which means of course that one in forty cars may be wrongly identified. (I know this from personal experience as the plate of one car I was driving was incorrectly read, and the car was falsely flagged as stolen!)

1977 Volvo 240 (Bengt Ericsson CC SA 3.0 via Wikimedia Commons)

1977: THE FIRST DAYTIME RUNNING LIGHTS

Daytime running lights have been controversial ever since their introduction over forty years ago. Scandinavian countries were the first to require daytime running lights, motivated by very short winter daylight hours. Sweden was first in 1977, and the Volvo 240 was the first car in the world equipped as such. Norway followed in 1986, Iceland in 1988 and Denmark in 1990. Canada has also required these lights on all new cars since 1989. A by-product of this has been that in the US all the major manufacturers now install daytime running lights on all models because the cost of having two versions of a model, one for the States and one for Canada, is excessive.

1980: THE FIRST DRIVERLESS CARS

The prospect of driverless cars on our roads excites some but horrifies many. It sounds like pure science fiction. Most people assume it is a very recent phenomenon, but in fact the idea has been pursued for nearly forty years. Developments have gone through two phases: firstly there were cars designed to follow wires buried in the road, following defined routes, rather like trolley buses, then there were cars designed to be completely autonomous which interpret road features like a human driver.

The first experiments with wire-guided cars were undertaken by the Radio Corporation of America (RCA) in 1953 using scale models. Tests with full-sized cars began in 1957 on a section of US Route 77, although in these tests the wire guidance was assisted by an optical system which detected lights set at the side of the road. In the UK, the Transport and Road Research Laboratory was testing wire-guided systems using magnetic cables under the road surface.

Research on wire-guided systems continued into the 1970s, but systems with wires and guiding lights could hardly have been called truly driverless. The first 'proper' fully autonomous vehicle didn't appear until 1980, when a Mercedes-Benz van, equipped with vision guidance, achieved speeds of up to 39mph on a public road closed to other traffic. This was the work of Ernst Dickmanns and his team at the Bundeswehr University in Munich, Germany. But this was still a long way off a driverless car which can cope with pedestrians and other cars.

1980: KEYLESS ENTRY

The very first keyless entry consisted of a numeric key pad mounted on the driver's door above the door handle. Ford introduced what they called SecuriCode on their Thunderbird, Mercury Cougar, Lincoln Continental and Lincoln Town Car in 1980. Nissan followed a similar route in 1984 with their Maxima and Fairlady models, but added further features on the key pad including opening windows and the moon-roof, and installed keypads on both front doors. Subaru followed an entirely different route, whereby the door could be unlocked by pulling the driver's door handle a specific number of times to enter a pass-code number. All these approaches were soon overtaken by the radio-frequency remote control, which is almost universal today. The first radio remote appeared as standard fitment on Renault's Fuego model in 1982.

1980: VARIABLE VALVE TIMING

Up until the 1950s or 1960s there was little need for variable valve timing (VVT) for normal road cars. Engine speeds at the time rarely exceeded 5,000rpm. But as higher engine speeds became more common, the benefits of altering the valve timing became more apparent. The first car company to patent a VVT system was Fiat in the late 1960s. This system combined variable timing with variable valve lift, giving a double benefit.

1982 Renault Fuego (Furtivoman CC SA 4.0 via Wikimedia Commons)

1980 Alfa Romeo Spider 2000 (Alf van Beem CC 1.0 via Wikimedia Commons)

It was developed for Fiat by Giovanni Torazza and used hydraulic pressure to vary the fulcrum of the cam followers. The first production car to use this system was the 1980 Alfa Romeo Spider 2000, Alfa being part of the Fiat Group. In 1987 Nissan introduced a more sophisticated electronic VVT system which they called 'NVCS', and in 1989 Honda launched their 'VTEC' system. These two systems work in different ways. Nissan's NVCS system alters the phasing of the camshaft, whereas Honda's VTEC system switches the valves onto a different cam profile at high engine speeds. Honda first introduced their VTEC system in their Civic, CTX and Integra models in Japan and Europe.

1983: THE FIRST START-STOP

Start-stop technology first appeared in Europe, spurred on by high fuel prices and concerns about pollution from idling cars. In addition, 25 per cent of the New European Driving Cycle (NEDC) – used to assess urban fuel consumption – is spent idling, so stop-start helps boost claimable fuel economy considerably. The first car fitted with stop-start as standard was the Volkswagen Polo Formel E in 1983. Soon the system was also being fitted to Polo, Passat and Golf Bluemotion models. Fiat was the second company to apply the technology, starting in 1984 with their Lupo 3L model. The technology was much later in arriving in the US (2012) and Japan (1997). In the US, there was initially quite a lot of resistance to the technology on the grounds that it was irritating, that it could potentially lead to premature engine wear and that fuel was cheap anyway.

1983: THE FIRST TRACTION CONTROL

Traction control is a system designed to prevent wheels spinning uncontrollably when they lose grip, by applying controlled braking to the spinning wheel until it comes back under control. This is to be distinguished from the more advanced Electronic Stability Control (*see* 1990) which goes one step further by allocating power to different wheels in such a way as to maximise stability. The first traction control system in a production car was seen in the 1983 Toyota Crown which featured a 'four-wheel electronic anti-skid control system'. In 1987 both BMW and Mercedes-Benz introduced their first traction-control systems, since when traction control, often as part of a more comprehensive stability control system, has become 'mainstream'.

1985: THE FIRST HEATED WINDSCREEN

The first heated windscreens were introduced by Ford in 1985 in the US on the Ford Taunus/Mercury Sable and in Europe on the Ford Scorpio/Granada Mk III. In early promotional sales literature for Europe the feature was referred to simply as Rapid Windscreen De-ice, but the Quickclear name began to appear from around 1989 onwards. The system can now be found as either standard equipment or an optional extra on most vehicles produced by Ford or its subsidiaries around the

1983 Toyota Crown

world, but in the US market it was never popular. It appeared also in some Land Rovers and Jaguars during and after Ford ownership.

The system uses a mesh of very thin heating wires, or a silver/zinc oxide coated film embedded between two layers of windscreen glass. The overall effect when operative was defogging and defrosting of the windscreen at a very high rate. Because of the high current draw, the system is engineered to operate only when the engine is running, and normally switches off after ten minutes of operation. General Motors has developed a similar system called Electriclear.

1989: THE FIRST HEAD-UP DISPLAY

Head-up displays first appeared for the general public in 1989 with Nissan offering the feature on their 240SX, and General Motors on their Cutlass Supreme and Pontiac Grand Prix models, having trialled them the previous year on their Indy Pace Cars only. Toyota followed in 1991 on their Crown Majesta model, whilst the first colour display appeared on the 1998 Chevrolet Corvette.

1990: THE FIRST ELECTRONIC STABILITY CONTROL

Electronic Stability Control takes the idea of traction control one step further. Whereas traction control uses the brakes to prevent wheels spinning uncontrollably, and thereby reducing the risk of a skid, electronic stability control redistributes power between wheels to keep the vehicle going in the intended direction as indicated by the position of the steering wheel. All electronic stability control systems provide traction control, but not all traction control systems provide stability control. The first fully integrated stability control system appeared in 1990 when Mitsubishi

1990 Mitsubishi Sigma (Automodeller, CC SA 3.0)

launched the Diamante (Sigma) on the domestic Japanese market. It featured a new electronically controlled active trace and traction control system, the first integration of these two systems in the world. Various related systems have now developed from this start, with BMW applying a torque control system on all models from 1992. Audi introduced the first series 'ESP' on their 'quattro' cars and Volvo had a similar system on their S80, launched in 1998.

1992: THE FIRST CARBON-FIBRE MONOCOQUE

Today a host of 'hyper cars', including Pagani, Koenigsegg, Lamborghini and Ferrari, have models utilising a carbon-fibre monocoque. Racing cars have been using this technique for some time. The first production car so constructed was the McLaren F1 in 1992. This used magnesium and aluminium attachments set into the carbon-fibre shell to connect to the suspension. However, the engine bay itself was not made from carbon fibre because the high temperature variations can cause mechanical stress over time.

1994: THE FIRST ALUMINIUM SPACE FRAME

Although some sources claim the Stout Scarab had the first aluminium space frame, this is untrue. The first Scarab of 1932 had aluminium body panels, but the structural frame was steel. We have to scroll forward sixty-two years to find the first production car with an aluminium space frame. The Audi A8 launched in 1994 featured a full Aluminium Space Frame (ASF) chassis, claimed to be 40 per cent lighter yet 40 per cent stiffer than a steel equivalent. The Audi A2 employed the second generation of ASF technology, which

1994 Audi A8 (Mhueltner CC SA 4.0 via Wikimedia Commons)

1992 McLaren F1 (Joe Cheng CC 2.0 via Wikimedia Commons)

involved larger but fewer frames, hence fewer nodes which required less welding. Laser welding was also used extensively in the bonding. All this helped to reduce the production costfor the cheaper A2. Jaguar adopted a full aluminium space frame for their XJ model in 2009, with the aluminium components largely glued together rather than welded or riveted.

1997: THE FIRST V5 ENGINE

The Volkswagen Group introduced the first V5 engine in 1997 in the Passat, and then later the same year in the Golf and Bora. These had a 2.3-litre 148bhp V5 engine which had a very narrow 15-degree V angle and a single-cylinder head and single camshaft. It was derived from Volkswagen's V6 engine by removing one cylinder. In 2000 the head was updated with twin cams and twenty variable-time valves, raising the power to 168bhp. The engine was noted for its interesting 'warbling' sound. As early as 1983 Oldsmobile developed a V5 diesel engine, but it never went into production.

Twenty-First-Century Firsts

2003: THE FIRST PARKING SENSORS

Parking sensors may be thought of as a recent innovation, but the technology has been around since the 1970s. Originally, they were developed to be used in guidance devices for the blind or partially sighted. It wasn't until the early 2000s that the technology was applied to the automobile, and the first mainstream volume production car to feature the technology was the 2003 Toyota Prius. Parking sensors use ultrasonic technology and are installed in the bumpers of the car. They can 'sense' the surroundings and measure the distance between the car and obstacles on the road. The driver is warned via a beeping noise which becomes more rapid the closer their car gets to an object. Usually, the sound is accompanied by a digital graphic on the dashboard which shows the distance more accurately. Sensors are the most basic and most common parking system.

2006: THE FIRST SMART MOTORWAY (FREEWAY)

The idea behind a 'smart' motorway is that information constantly collected about traffic flows, obstructions, weather conditions, etc., is used to manage traffic movement. This is achieved through variable speed limits, hard-shoulder running, closing and opening lanes, and a variety of other directions communicated to drivers. It is sometimes called Active Traffic Management (ATM). The benefits are intended to be smoother flows, less bunching, more reliable travel times, lower emissions as a result of fewer start/stops and reduced noise. The technique was first used in the UK on the M42 motorway in the West Midlands in 2006. A higher speed limit of 60mph was trialled on the southbound carriageway between junctions 4 and 3A from 2008, a 10mph increase on the previous maximum permissible speed. In 2007 plans were announced to extend the scheme to two sections of the M6 near Birmingham. The United States began exploring the use of ATM techniques somewhat later, in 2016.

The First Cars by Country

Finally, it is interesting to contrast the date of the birth of the automobile industry in different countries with the current scale of passenger-car production. In 2016 production of passenger cars in the top six producing countries was as follows:

- *China*   24.42 million
- *Japan*   7.78 million
- Germany   5.75 million
- United States   3.93 million
- *South Korea*   3.86 million
- *India*   3.67 million

Yet if we look at the date the first cars were made in various countries we see an enormous difference. These are some of the countries producing cars earliest, together with the four (shown in *italics* in the above list) who started much later:

1886	Germany with the Benz
1891	France with the Panhard et Levassor
1893	United States with the Duryea
1896	Russia with the Yakolev & Freze
1899	Italy with the Fiat 4hp
1907	Japan with the Takuri from Komanosuke Uchiyama
1942	India with the Hindustan Ambassador
1958	China with the Hongqi CA72
1975	South Korea with the Hyundai Pony

The rapid ascendance of India, China and South Korea is starkly highlighted, as to a lesser extent is Japan. Of the early pioneers, France (1.63m), Russia (1.12m) and Italy (0.71m) are now relatively minor producers on the world stage.

Clockwise from left: 1959 Hongqi CA72 (Navigator84 CC SA 3.0 via Wikimedia Commons); 1899 Fiat 3.5hp; 1895 Duryea (Buch-t CC SA 3.0 Germany via Wikimedia Commons)

1896 Yakolev & Free

Clockwise from above: 1891 Panhard et Levassor (P.poschadel CC SA 3.0 via Wikimedia Commons); 1895 Lanchester; 1886 Benz (CapCase CC 2.0 via Wikimedia Commons); 1975 Hyundai Pony (Free Photo Fun CC 2.0 via Wikimedia Commons)

1942 Hindustan Ambassador (calfier001 CC 2.0 via Wikimedia Commons)